THE BEST OF
The
MAILBOX®
Magazine

Arts and Crafts

GRADES 1–3

Find just the arts-and-crafts idea you need when you need it with *The Best of* The Mailbox® *Arts and Crafts*. The ideas and activities included were originally published in *The* Primary *Mailbox* magazine between October/November 1993 and June/July 1998.

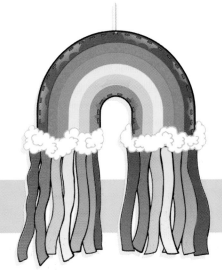

Editor:
Karen A. Brudnak

Artists:
Pam Crane, Teresa R. Davidson, Sheila Krill,
Becky Saunders, Barry Slate

Cover Artist:
Kimberly Richard

www.themailbox.com

©1999 by THE EDUCATION CENTER, INC.
All rights reserved.
ISBN #1-56234-324-6

Manufactured in the United States
10 9 8 7 6 5 4 3 2

Table of Contents

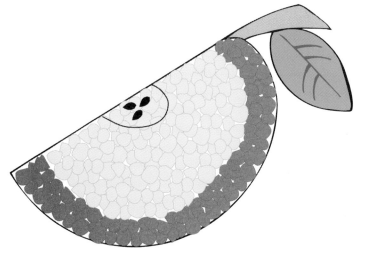

Easy Art Tips

No-Fuss Window Displays

The next time you display student artwork on the windows, grab your glue stick. Use the stick to dab glue on one side of the student paper; then immediately press the paper to the window. When it's time to change the display, simply peel the projects from the windows and wipe away any traces of leftover glue with a quick squirt of window cleaner. Quick and clean!

Linda Sanders—Gr. 3
Roseland Park Elementary
Picayune, MS

Bag It!

Pieces from an unfinished art project easily can be lost. Here's the perfect way to keep them safe. Attach a magnetic or self-adhesive cup hook to each child's desk. Then gather a resealable plastic bag for each student. Punch a hole in each bag and label it with a student's name. When it's time to clean up, have students place the pieces of their unfinished projects inside their bags and hang them on the hooks. No more missing parts!

Ann Margaret Neal—Gr. 2
Encino Park Elementary
San Antonio, TX

Clog No More

Eliminate clogged glue bottles for good! Here's how. Remove the protective cap from an unused glue container. Use a cotton swab covered in Vaseline® to coat the inside of the cap. Also coat the cap's exposed tip before snapping the cap back in place. Say good-bye to the pesky problem of clogged caps!

Betty Lynn Scholtz—Gr. 1
Providence Day School
Charlotte, NC

Placemat Patterns

Are your tagboard templates ragged around the edges from frequent use? Replace those old favorites with templates cut from inexpensive vinyl placemats. Vinyl templates hold their shape for years of classroom use, so you won't need to spend time replacing worn-out patterns!

Cheryl Pilgrim
San Antonio, TX

Crayon Canisters

Reunite lost crayons and their owners with this colorful idea. Cover eight same-size containers with different colors of construction paper representing the eight basic colors. Place the canisters in a convenient location. When a child finds a lost crayon, she drops it into the corresponding canister. When the owner discovers that a crayon is missing from her box, she takes one from the color-coded canisters. A perfect match!

Jo Bowman—Gr. 1
Caloosa Elementary
Cape Coral, FL

Clever Cleanup

Arts-and-crafts activities are fun, but they can lead to a messy classroom. Enlist the help of litter-eating Egabrag (*garbage* spelled backward). Cut the shape of a dust ball from gray construction paper; then add facial features and the message "Please feed Egabrag!" Use clear Con-Tact® covering to attach the cutout to your classroom trash can. When you see signs of classroom litter, a gentle reminder such as "Did I just hear Egabrag's tummy growl?" will have students cleaning up in no time!

Jo Fryer—Gr. 1
Kildeer Countryside School
Long Grove, IL

Apple Baskets

Weave these personalized apple baskets into your back-to-school plans. To begin, fold a 9" x 12" sheet of construction paper in half (to 9" x 6"). At the end opposite the fold, cut away a 1" x 8" strip from both thicknesses as shown. Then, keeping the paper folded and starting at the fold, cut a series of one-inch strips, stopping approximately one inch from the open ends. Unfold the resulting loom and weave seven or eight one-inch construction-paper strips in the loom. When all the strips are woven, glue the ends of each woven strip in place. To personalize the basket, trace and cut out the letters needed from construction paper. Glue the letters in a pleasing arrangement on the woven basket. Next cut five apple shapes from red paper. Glue the apple cutouts near the top of the basket; then label each one with a self-describing adjective. Attach green leaves and brown stems to the apples if desired. Display the completed projects on a bulletin board titled "A Bushel Of Good Apples!"

adapted from an idea by Teri Eklund—Gr. 2
Walker Elementary, Springdale, AR

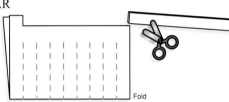

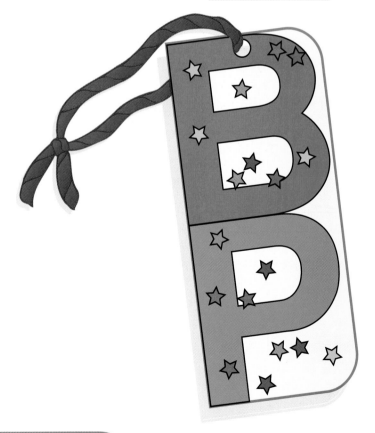

Back-To-School Bookmarks

Make reading a top priority this year with personalized bookmarks! To make a bookmark, trace and cut out the beginning letters of your first and last names from colorful paper. Next cut two 4" x 9" rectangles from clear Con-Tact® covering. Peel the backing from one rectangle. Arrange the letter cutouts on the adhesive; then sprinkle the adhesive with colorful glitter, confetti, or small paper punches. Peel the backing from the second rectangle and align the rectangle—adhesive side down—atop the project. Trim the edges of the resulting bookmark to create a preferred shape. If desired, punch a hole in the top of the bookmark and tie a loop of yarn through the hole.

Jo Fryer, Kildeer Countryside School, Long Grove, IL

Sparkling Apples

You don't have to shake a tree limb to get great apples! Shake some salt instead. Mix equal amounts of red powdered tempera paint and salt. Pour the mixture into an empty spice container that has a top with small holes, or pour it into an empty salt shaker. Prepare containers of green- and yellow-tinted salt in the same manner. Using a wide paintbrush, coat a tagboard apple cutout with water-thinned glue. Select one (or more) shakers and sprinkle tinted salt onto the glue. When the glue is dry, shake off the excess salt. If desired, trim student work to fit the back of each apple cutout before suspending the apples from the ceiling.

Valerie Lathrop, Glendale, AZ

Pretty Patchwork Apples

Johnny Appleseed would have to agree—these pretty patchwork apples are definitely the pick of the crop! Start with a large, tagboard apple cutout (pattern on page 93) and a supply of two-inch fabric squares. Using a paintbrush, brush a thin coating of glue on the back of a fabric square; then press the square of fabric onto the apple cutout. Continue in this manner, slightly overlapping the fabric squares, until the entire apple cutout is covered. Let the project dry overnight; then trim away any fabric that extends beyond the tagboard cutout. Attach a brown stem and a green leaf (patterns on page 93) to complete the project.

Donna Oldfield—Gr. 1
Portsmouth Catholic School
Portsmouth, VA

Squirrel's Nest

If your youngsters get a kick out of watching squirrels collect acorns, they'll have a lot of fun creating these squirrelly critters. To make an imitation squirrel's nest, begin by rolling down the top of a brown paper bag about two-thirds of the way. Color a white construction-paper copy of the squirrel on page 94, and cut it out along the bold lines. Fold the cutout along the dotted lines so that the squirrel will be two-sided and self-standing. Tape or glue the flaps that are below the squirrel's body to the inside bottom of the bag. Tape or glue leaves to cover the exterior of the bag, and place additional leaves inside the bag around the squirrel. Put a few acorns around the squirrel to represent his personal winter stash.

Peg Meehan, Narragansett, RI

Who's Who?

Students provide the clues for this clever project that's a must for Open House! To make the handprints, prepare a mixture of tempera paint and liquid soap for each desired paint color. Then, using a paintbrush, brush a thin layer of paint on a student's palms before she presses them onto white fingerpaint paper. Set this part of the project aside to dry. Next each child uses fabric scraps, construction paper and yarn, markers, crayons, glue, and a paper plate to create a self-likeness. She then completes a set of clues like the ones shown. Finally each youngster cuts out her handprints and assembles her project on a 12" x 18" sheet of black paper. Display the mysterious projects on a bulletin board titled "Guess Who?"

Teri Eklund—Gr. 2
Walker Elementary
Springdale, AR

I have _blue_ eyes.
I have _brown_ hair.
I am a _girl_.
I love to _dance_.
Who am I?

Fall Foliage

Stick with this idea to create a spectacular display of fall foliage! To make a large fall leaf, begin with a ten-inch square of clear Con-Tact® covering. Remove the backing and place the covering sticky side up on a tabletop. Completely cover the sticky surface with torn pieces of tissue paper in assorted fall colors—being sure to overlap the tissue-paper pieces. Use a spray bottle or an eyedropper filled with water to dampen the tissue paper, which makes the colors bleed. Let the project dry overnight; then remove the backing from a second ten-inch square of clear Con-Tact® covering and align the covering atop the tissue paper. Cut a large leaf shape from the project. For a spectacular fall display, punch a hole near the top of each leaf cutout and use monofilament line to suspend the shapes from the ceiling.

Tony Johnson—Gr. 3, Danvers Elementary, Danvers, IL

Colorful Leaf Prints

Be prepared for plenty of oohhhs and ahhhhhs as these leaf-print projects take shape. Enlist your students' help in gathering a supply of fallen leaves. Encourage students to look for large leaves in a variety of shapes. Partially fill each of several shallow containers with a different fall-colored tempera paint (orange, yellow, red, green, brown). To begin, lay a leaf on a paper-covered surface so that its rough side is facing upward. Then, using a paintbrush and the provided paints, paint the rough side of the leaf. Use one or several colors of paint, making sure to cover the entire leaf surface. Carefully pick up the painted leaf and flip it over onto a sheet of white paper. Use one hand to securely hold the leaf in place. Use the fingers of your other hand to gently rub the entire unpainted leaf surface. Then carefully lift the leaf off the paper and set the resulting leaf print aside to dry. To complete the project, trim the leaf print and mount it on a slightly larger piece of fall-colored construction paper. Trim the construction paper to create an eye-catching border.

Ann Flagg, Clarion, PA

Dramatic Display

Create a dramatic fall-foliage display with these colorful construction-paper leaves. Partially fill each of several shallow containers with fall-colored powdered tempera paint (orange, red, yellow, green, brown). Then, working atop a newspaper-covered surface, cover a 9" x 12" sheet of fall-colored construction paper with irregular paint splotches. To do this, dip a wet paintbrush into a container of powdered paint and splotch the paint onto the construction paper. Clean the brush; then repeat the painting step—using a variety of paint colors—until a desired effect is achieved. When the paint has dried, trim the painted paper into the shape of a large leaf. Laminate the leaves if desired; then display them as embellishments or borders on classroom bulletin boards.

Camilla Law—Gr. 3, St. Timothy's School, Raleigh, NC

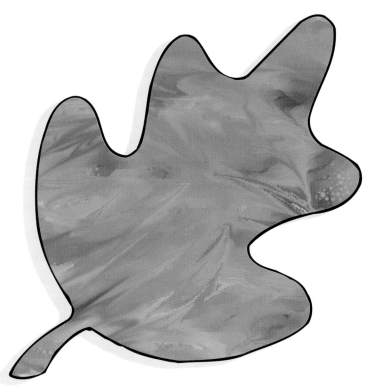

Tree Weavings

Weave some red, orange, and yellow into green paper foliage to bring the first touches of autumn color into your classroom. To make one of these trees, begin by cutting a sheet of green construction paper to resemble the foliage of a deciduous tree. Fold this paper cutout in the middle. Use a ruler to draw parallel lines from the fold to within an inch of the opposite edges of the paper, spacing the lines about one-half inch apart. Cut on the lines; then unfold the paper. Weave 1/2" x 9" strips of red, orange, and yellow paper through the slits in the green paper. Glue the strips' ends to the green paper before trimming away any unattached parts of the strips. Use glue to attach a brown construction-paper trunk cutout to the woven foliage.

Vicki Smith, Murfreesboro, TN

Fall Leaf Banner

Enlist your students' help in collecting colorful autumn leaves for this project. To make a banner, fold a three-foot length of waxed paper in half; then unfold the paper. Brush one half of the paper with a layer of thinned white glue. Place pieces of torn tissue paper on the glue so that they overlap. Next arrange several fall leaves atop the tissue-paper design. Cover the project with the remaining half of the waxed paper. Sandwich the project between newsprint, and press it with an iron on low heat.

To display the project, fold a 9" x 12" sheet of construction paper lengthwise. Unfold the paper. Run a trail of glue from corner to corner as shown. Lay the midsection of a three-foot length of yarn in the crease of the paper so that equal lengths of yarn extend on the sides. Then refold the paper, tucking one narrow end of the waxed-paper project inside. Tie the yarn ends and suspend the resulting banner for all to see.

Linda Rabinowitz—Gr. 1, Torah Day School Of Atlanta, Atlanta, GA

glue

yarn

Leaves Everywhere

Create the image of falling leaves with this art project. To begin, cut a tree trunk shape from brown construction paper and glue it to a sheet of black paper. Align red, orange, yellow, and green strips of construction paper and hold them in one hand. Then cut the strips to create a pile of triangular pieces. Glue the triangles onto the black construction paper for the tree's foliage. Glue some leaves to the tree trunk, some on the ground, and some in the air. It's a bright blizzard of leaves!

Vida Vaitkus—Gr. 3, Marvin School, Stratford, CT

Jack-O'-Lantern Trio

By Jove! It is three jack-o'-lanterns! For this project, fold each of three 12-inch squares of orange construction paper in half. Make a half-pumpkin template similar to the one shown. Cut out the template and trace it on each folded square. Cut on the resulting lines; then unfold the squares to reveal three pumpkin shapes. From scrap paper, cut out desired facial features and stems. Glue the cutouts in place. When the glue has dried, refold the pumpkins, making sure that the artwork is folded to the inside.

To assemble the project, place one folded pumpkin shape on a tabletop. Apply a thin coat of glue on the upper paper surface. Lay one end of a crepe-paper streamer near the bottom edge. Then, lining up the edges, place another folded pumpkin shape atop the first one. Repeat the process, this time aligning the third folded shape atop the second one. Next cover the upper paper surface of the third pumpkin with glue. Position a crepe-paper streamer as before; then carefully pick up the project and bring together the top and bottom surfaces. Hole-punch the pumpkin stem; then thread and tie a few lengths of curled ribbon through the stem. Suspend the project from monofilament line. Now that's a handsome threesome!

Cynthia Goth—Gr. 1, Glen Elder Grade School, Glen Elder, KS

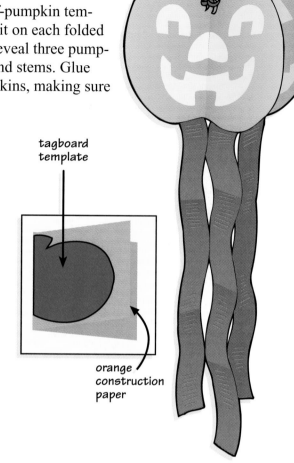

tagboard template

orange construction paper

Spooky Specters

Your youngsters will hardly believe their eyes when they see the results of this spirited art project. To begin, bend a white clothes hanger into any ghostly shape. Stretch one leg of a pair of white pantyhose over the hanger, pulling it toward the hook of the hanger. At the base of the hook, secure the hose with a piece of white yarn. Cut eyes and other facial features from construction paper. Glue them to the hose. Hang these spooky ghosts by their hooks when the glue is thoroughly dry.

Laurie Vent, Upper Sandusky, OH

Spooky Windsocks

Dangle these projects from your classroom ceiling to create a bewitchingly whimsical effect. Roll a 6" x 18" strip of purple construction paper into a cylinder and glue the overlapping edges together. Set the cylinder aside to dry. Fashion two or more Halloween decorations from colorful scraps of construction paper, using crayons or markers to add desired details. Or provide seasonally shaped stencils for students to trace on construction paper, cut out, and decorate. Glue the completed decorations on the cylinder. Glue six 16-inch strips of colorful crepe paper inside the lower rim of the project. To prepare the project for hanging, punch two holes near the top of the cylinder so that the holes are on opposite sides of the project. Thread each end of a 16-inch length of yarn through a different hole and securely tie.

Jeri Daugherity—Gr. 1
Mother Seton School
Emmitsburg, MD

Paper-Bag Haunts

For this spooky project, students decorate a paper bag to resemble a haunted house. To begin, partially fill a lunch bag with crumpled newspaper; then fold down and staple the top of the bag closed. To make the roof, decorate a construction-paper rectangle and fold it in half. Partially unfold the paper and attach it to the top of the bag. Use construction-paper scraps, glue, markers, crayons, and other desired supplies to create a front door that swings open, windows and shutters, a chimney, and other haunted-house decorations—including several ghoulish houseguests!

VaReane Gray Heese, Omaha, NE

Eight-Legged Look-Alikes

Send your spider enthusiasts into a spin with this adorable arachnid! Use black tempera paint to cover both sides of a small-size paper soup bowl. Set the bowl aside to dry. To make the spider's legs, accordion-fold eight 1" x 8" black paper strips. Also cut out and decorate two colorful construction-paper eyes. When the painted bowl is dry, attach the eyes and legs to it as shown. Knot one end of a long length of elastic thread. Thread the unknotted end of elastic through a needle; then poke the needle through the center of the bowl so that the knot remains inside the bowl. Display the three-dimensional spiders where they can spin and sway in the cool October breezes.

Cindy Schumacher—Gr. 1
Prairie Elementary School
Cottonwood, ID

Haunted House

There's not a ghost of a chance that your youngsters will boo this art project! Begin by sketching the outline of a large, spooky-looking house on a page of classified ads. Cut out the shape; then snip and fold open a desired number of doors and windows. Mount the cutout on a 12" x 18" sheet of dark-colored construction paper. Now the real fun begins! Using construction-paper scraps, glue, markers, crayons, and other desired supplies, create spooky scenery and a house full of ghoulish guests! Boo!

Gobble! Gobble!

This November create a flock of "hand-some" gobblers! To make one of the gobblers, trace the outline of your shoe onto brown construction paper. Also trace the outline of your hand (fingers outstretched) onto sheets of red, blue, purple, orange, green, and yellow construction paper. Cut along the resulting outlines. Position the cutout that matches your shoe's sole so that the heel is at the top and will represent the turkey's head. Glue eyes, a beak, a wattle, and feet cut from construction paper to the turkey body. Stack the hand cutouts; then fan them out to create a colorful set of tail feathers. Glue the feathers to the back of the turkey. Just look at that turkey strut!

Mosaic Placemats

Students will be delighted to add these placemats to their Thanksgiving dinner plans. Cut a supply of one-inch squares from brown, yellow, red, green, orange, and purple construction paper. To make a placemat, trace a large cornucopia-shaped template onto a 12" x 18" sheet of white construction paper. Arrange and glue brown paper squares to cover the horn-shaped basket; then arrange and glue the colorful paper squares to create an assortment of fruit shapes spilling from the basket. Use markers to add a holiday greeting; then sign and date the back of the project. For durability laminate the resulting placemat or cover it with clear Con-Tact® covering. Happy Thanksgiving!

Betsy Ruggiano—Gr. 3, Featherbed Lane School, Clark, NJ

Adorable Snow Pals

Even if snow isn't in the forecast, your students will have plenty of frosty fun creating these three-dimensional snow pals! For artistic inspiration, read aloud *Snowballs* by Lois Ehlert (Harcourt Brace & Company, 1995). Then give each child two sheets of 12" x 18" construction paper—one white and one blue. Also make available incrementally sized circle templates for optional student use. A student cuts out and mounts a white construction-paper snow pal onto his blue paper. Then he hole-punches his scrap paper and glues the resulting snowflakes to his project.

At this point, set the projects aside and revisit Lois Ehlert's book, focusing on the variety of snow-pal decorations the illustrator uses. Make plans to decorate the snow-pal projects the following day and invite students to bring from home a variety of decorating items. Also have on hand items like popcorn kernels, popped corn, raisins, buttons, small washers, sunflower seeds, construction-paper scraps, and discarded magazines for student use. Display the decorated snow pals in a hallway for others to admire!

Susie Kapaun, Littleton, CO

Snazzy Snowflakes

Create a flurry of snazzy snowflakes without a lot of fuss! Begin by demonstrating how to make a snowflake by folding, cutting, and unfolding a paper square. While students are honing their snowflake-making skills (using recycled paper squares), pour a thin layer of white tempera paint into a jelly-roll pan. Add a squirt of liquid soap to the paint for easier cleanup.

To make a snazzy snowflake like the one shown, cut a snowflake from a five-inch square of white construction paper. Glue the snowflake near the center of a 12" x 18" sheet of blue construction paper. Press your opened palm into the paint; then repeatedly press it around the edges of the mounted snowflake as shown—reapplying paint as needed. When the project is dry, trim away any excess blue paper and display the one-of-a-kind snowflake. Let it snow!

Theresa Cox—Gr. 1, Fisher Grade School, Fisher, IL

Parka Pals

When the temperature drops, slip into this parka project and watch students' interest go up and up. To make a parka pal, trace a circle template that's seven inches in diameter onto skin-toned paper. Cut on the resulting outline. Using markers, glue, scissors, construction paper, and assorted art supplies, decorate the circle to resemble your face. Glue the circle to a paper plate; then glue cotton balls along the outer rim of the plate. Trim to round two corners of a 9" x 12" sheet of construction paper, and draw two lines as shown to indicate the arms of the jacket. Glue this paper to the back of the plate. Complete this project by attaching buttons and/or cotton balls to finish the parka. It's cold outside, but you'd never know it snuggled deep down in your parka!

Deborah Burleson, Silverdale, WA

Penguins With A Personal Touch

Have you ever had a personal connection with a penguin? No? Well, here's your chance! To make a penguin, begin by tracing the outline of your hand (fingers outstretched) and your shoe onto black construction paper. Cut along the resulting outlines. Position the cutout that matches your shoe's sole so that the heel of the tracing is at the top and will represent the penguin's head. Use white chalk to color the penguin's belly. Split the hand cutout by cutting downward between the index and middle fingers. Glue the part with the thumb and index-finger shapes to the penguin's body so that it resembles its foot. Attach the remaining part of the hand cutout to the body to represent a flipper. Trace the end of your thumb onto orange construction paper. Cut on the outline and glue the cutout to the penguin so that it resembles the penguin's beak. Finish this proper penguin by attaching an eye fashioned from paper. How about that? You now have a personal connection with a penguin!

Melissa Raleigh—Gr. 1, Whittier Elementary School, Amarillo, TX

Amaryllis: Winter Color

Brighten winter days with these colorful flowers. Bunch six 3-inch lengths of yellow pipe cleaner; then twist together the bottom ends to form the flower's stamens. To create the flower petals, stack and fold into thirds, two 9" x 6" sheets of red tissue paper. Cut a petal shape from one end as shown. Unfold the paper and shift the top sheet so that the petal shapes alternate; then accordion-fold the base of the petals. Wrap the folded base around the twisted end of the stamens. Overlap the paper ends; then pinch the paper around the stamens and secure it with tape. Carefully bend the petals away from the stamens; then set the project aside.

To make the stem and leaves, you need three 2" x 16" strips of green paper. Roll one paper strip into a tube and secure the resulting stem with tape. Fold the remaining paper strips lengthwise; then trim one end of each strip to resemble a leaf. Attach the leaves to the base of the stem. Glue the stem and leaves to a 6" x 18" sheet of construction paper. Secure the base of the bloom inside the stem and gently tilt the bloom forward. To make a flowerpot, cut a trapezoid shape from foil wrapping paper and glue it over the base of the plant. If desired, glue a small amount of Spanish moss peeking out of the top of the pot.

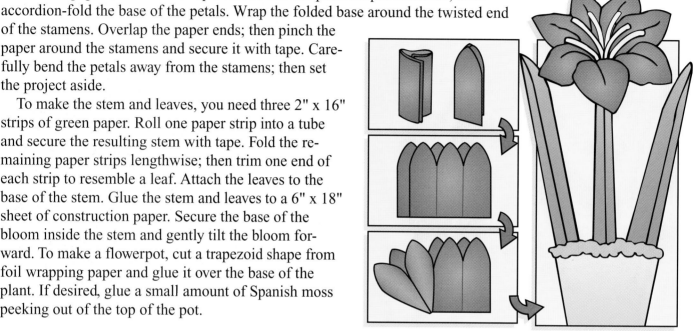

Snowflakes From Spaghetti

Follow these steps to create a flurry of colorful snowflakes. Pour an ample amount of white (or pastel-tinted) glue into a pie tin. Then, working atop a sheet of waxed paper, dip each of several cooked and cooled spaghetti noodles into the glue. Position the noodles in an abstract snowflake shape atop the waxed paper. Sprinkle your completed project with silver glitter and let it dry overnight. If desired suspend the shimmering flakes from the ceiling on lengths of monofilament line. Let it snow!

Karen Lyon—Gr. 1, Lenoir City Elementary, Lenoir City, TN

The Water's Fine!

Your youngsters will dive into this project with much the same enthusiasm that compels a penguin to plop blithely into frigid waters. To begin making the sky in this icy scene, use a wide brush to paint the upper half of a large sheet of art paper with water. Use thinned yellow tempera paint to make horizontal streaks in the wet area; then brush sweeping strokes of thinned red paint in some of the remaining moistened area. Observe as the colors bleed and mingle. Using the same wet-on-wet process, paint the entire lower half of the art paper with water first; then paint on streaks of thinned green and blue paint. When the paper has thoroughly dried, attach torn pieces of white construction paper with glue so that they appear to be icebergs floating in the water. Fashion a few penguins from construction paper and glue them to the scene. Mount the artwork on a larger sheet of blue paper. Wouldn't you just love to dive in?

Michelle Williams—Gr. 1, Meadow Lane School, Olathe, KS

Bag It!

For this neighborly project, students work independently to create paper lunch-bag dwellings, then pool their projects to create a neighborhood. To make a dwelling, partially fill a lunch bag with crumpled newspaper; then fold down and staple the top of the bag closed. To make a roof, decorate a construction-paper rectangle and fold it in half. Partially unfold the paper and attach it to the top of the bag. Use an assortment of craft supplies to create desired details like curtained windows, a front door, and a chimney. Mount this project on a 9" x 11" tagboard lot. Add landscaping features such as a lawn, trees, shrubs, a fence, and a sidewalk. For a snowy scene, pull apart several cotton balls and glue the fluffy snow in place.

To create a neighborhood, fashion streets from black paper. Arrange the dwellings along the streets. Encourage students to make street signs, cars, and a neighborhood park and/or school. If possible, display the completed neighborhood scene in a central location so that the whole school can appreciate this community project!

Julie Rezash—Gr. 3, Cooper Elementary, Milwaukee, WI

Frozen Paint On A Stick

Warm up your youngsters on a wintry day with this unique painting project. At least one day in advance, prepare paint in several different colors for freezing. For each color, mix six tablespoons of powdered tempera paint with one cup of water. (For shimmery paint, stir a teaspoon of glitter into the solution.) Pour the paint solution into a large, wax-coated paper cup. Prop a wooden Popsicle® stick in the center of the cup; then freeze the cups overnight. To use the paints, dip the bottom half of each cup in a pan of warm water; then pull the "paintsicle" from the cup. Prop the paintsicles in a shallow container. Working atop newspaper, have students use the paintsicles to paint freestyle on finger-paint paper. If desired, have students place a textured surface, such as a sheet of corrugated cardboard or a window screen, under their projects as they paint. When the projects are dry, have each student trim his project into an interesting shape, then mount the cutout onto a slightly larger sheet of construction paper. After he trims the construction paper to create an eye-catching border, mount his project in your classroom art gallery. Move over, Picasso!

Glistening Winter Scene

This nifty winter project can transform any classroom from bland to "blizzard-ly." Pressing heavily, use crayons to draw a winter scene onto a white paper plate; then brush over the paper plate with diluted blue tempera paint. When the paint is dry, brush over the surface again, this time using diluted glue. Quickly sprinkle white glitter atop the plate before the glue dries. Shake the loose glitter from the project and display it as desired. Too cool!

Martha Hunsel Blank—Gr. 2
Fairmount School
St. Peters, MO

Frosty's Back!

Well, Frosty promised he'd return one day, and he's back in grand style! Depending on the ability level of your children, you may want to have students make the different parts of this snow pal over a series of days, then assemble the parts on another day.

To make the body and head:
1. Use a template to trace a large doughnut shape onto a 12-inch square of white construction paper.
2. Cut along the resulting outer line; then make a diagonal cut through the ring and cut along the inner line—creating one body and one head.
3. Repeat Steps 1 and 2.

To make the face:
1. Stack and trim two 1 1/2" squares of black paper to create two eyes.
2. Cut a nose shape from a scrap of orange paper.
3. Hole-punch a scrap of red paper. Use the resulting dots to form a mouth.
4. Glue the eyes, nose, and mouth cutouts in place.
5. Use pink chalk (or a pink crayon) to create rosy cheeks.

To make the hat:
1. Stack two 6" x 9" black paper rectangles and cut out a desired hat shape.

To make the mittens:
1. Stack two 4" x 5" blue paper rectangles and cut out a desired mitten shape.
2. Repeat Step 1.

To make the buttons:
1. Stack and trim two 2-inch squares to create one set of buttons.
2. Repeat Step 1 two more times.
3. Decorate the six resulting buttons as desired.

To make the scarf:
1. Color a similar design on each of two 3" x 12" strips of white paper.

To assemble and complete the snow pal:
1. Glue each set of buttons back-to-back, sandwiching one end of a 4-foot length of yarn between the cutouts.
2. Glue the body rings together, sandwiching the yarn and two very thin twigs between the layers.
3. Glue the head cutouts together, sandwiching the yarn and some of the body between the layers.
4. Glue the hat cutouts together, sandwiching the yarn and some of the head between the layers.
5. Glue the scarf cutouts together, sandwiching the snow pal's neck area between the layers. (When the glue has dried, cut fringe at the end of the scarf; then fold the scarf as shown.)
6. Glue each set of mitten cutouts back-to-back, sandwiching the end of a twig between each set.
7. Suspend the snow pal for all to see.

Theresa Cox—Gr. 1
Fisher Grade School
Fisher, IL

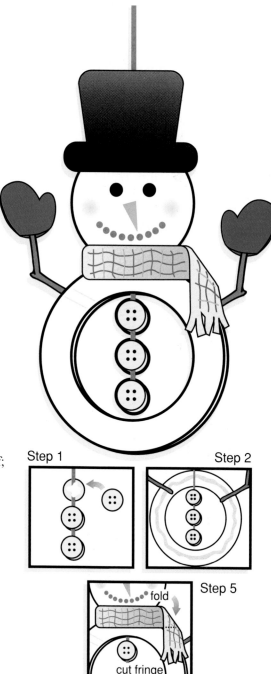

Step 1

Step 2

Step 5

fold

cut fringe

Swedish Holiday Fashions

Brighten your holiday festivities with a salute to Sweden's Festival Of Light (December 13), also known as St. Lucia Day.

Crown Of Candles

This leaf-covered crown of candles is traditionally worn by girls. To make a crown, use the patterns on page 97 to create five green construction-paper leaf shapes and five yellow candle flames. Cut out the patterns. Glue each flame cutout to a 1 1/2" x 4" strip of white construction paper to create a candle; then glue each candle to the straight end of a leaf cutout. Arrange the candle-adorned leaves end-to-end. Glue the pieces together by gluing a leaf tip over the bottom of each of the first four candles (see the illustration). When the glue has dried, size the resulting crown to fit the head of the intended wearer; then staple the crown ends together.

Star-Studded Hat

This cone-shaped hat is traditionally worn by Swedish boys. To make a hat, begin with a semicircle of white bulletin-board paper—diameter approximately 28 inches. Overlap the two corners of the paper until a cone is formed. Size the opening to fit the head of the intended wearer; then paper clip the overlapping edges of the hat rim. Tape the tip of the hat and trim away any extra paper; then remove the paper clip and securely glue the hat seam. Embellish the hat with yellow paper stars (pattern on page 97) and gold glitter.

Kathleen N. Kopp
Lecanto Primary School
Lecanto, FL

Warm Reminder

Crafted by little hands, this menorah project casts an especially warm, inviting light during Hanukkah. In preparation for making a menorah, position a sheet of construction paper horizontally and draw a centered horizontal line about two-thirds of the way down a sheet of construction paper. Extending upward from the line, draw nine evenly spaced, short, vertical lines, making the fifth one a bit longer than the others. Attach a sticky dot at the upper end of each vertical line. Use a marker to draw a base beneath the horizontal line to complete the menorah. For imitation candles, trim one swab from each of nine Q-tips®. Color each swab stick with a marker; then dip each swab in yellow paint. When the paint has dried, glue each swab to the menorah to resemble a candle. The cheerful glow of this menorah is a warm reminder of the great miracle it represents.

Ellen M. Stern—Gr. 1
Alberta Smith Elementary, Midlothian, VA

Holiday Prints

These one-of-a-kind holiday greeting cards leave lasting impressions. To make a card, fold a 9" x 12" sheet of construction paper in half; then set it aside. Cut a 6" x 9" rectangle from white art paper. Press a finger onto a brightly colored stamp pad and repeatedly press the ink-covered finger onto the art paper in a desired design. Continue in this fashion, using one or more colors. Trim around the completed project and mount it on the front of the folded paper. Write a holiday greeting on the front of the card and a holiday message inside the card.

Peg Daull
Christ The King School
East Cleveland, OH

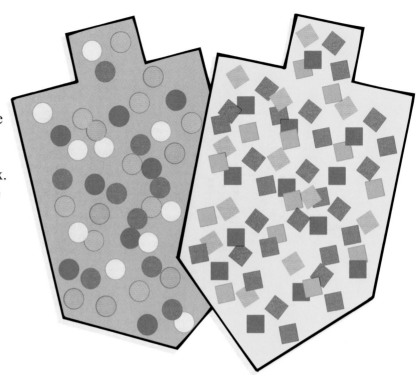

Decorative Dreidel

Keeping with the spirit and traditions of Hanukkah, have your youngsters create these festive dreidels. To make this project, begin with a dreidel cutout. Paint the cutout with thinned glue; then place it in a cardboard box. Sprinkle construction-paper confetti onto the dreidel cutout. Carefully lift the cutout from the box and tap off any loose confetti before setting the dreidel aside to dry.

Bernice Regenstein, Bricktown, NJ

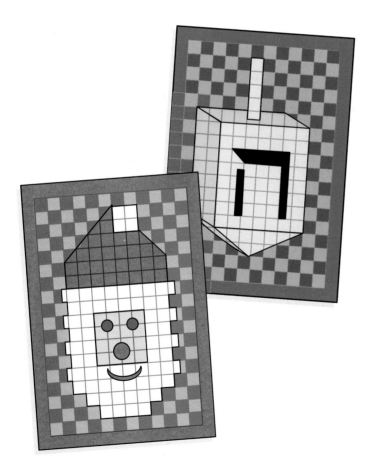

Creative Checks

Check this out! Here's a holiday art project that encourages creativity and requires minimal supplies! Begin with a 7" x 10" sheet of 1/2-inch graph paper. Using the lines as your guides, lightly sketch (in pencil) the outline of a desired holiday shape. Color the interior of the shape with markers or crayons; then use a black crayon to outline the shape and desired elements within the shape. Next choose two colors, and alternate between them to color each of the remaining squares on the page. When the page is completely colored, mount it onto a 9" x 12" sheet of colorful construction paper. "Check-tacular!"

Doris Hautala
Washington Elementary School, Ely, MN

Pretty Poinsettia Carryall

If you're into recycling, you're going to love making these colorful carryalls crafted from empty cereal boxes! Trim the top from an empty cereal box; then use tape and yellow paper to wrap the box—leaving the top of the box open. Trim several 2" x 3" red paper rectangles to resemble red poinsettia leaves, and two or more 3" x 4" green paper rectangles to resemble green poinsettia leaves. Glue the cutouts to the front of the paper-covered cereal box; then glue a smattering of yellow hole punches to the center of the resulting flower. To make a handle, hole-punch each narrow side of the carryall. Thread a 30-inch length of red or green curling ribbon through the holes and securely tie the ribbon ends. Pull the doubled-ribbon handle upward; then use a one-foot length of ribbon to tie the two handles together. Curl the ribbon ends. The colorful carryall can be suspended from a doorknob and used to store received greeting cards. Or it can be used as a holiday gift box.

Misti Craig—Gr. 1, Campbellsville Elementary School, Campbellsville, KY

Seasonal Symmetry

Stand back and watch the holiday season take shape as students create these colorful projects. Use the patterns on page 98 to create a desired number of seasonal templates. Begin with a 6" x 9" construction-paper rectangle and a 4 1/2" x 6" construction-paper rectangle in contrasting colors. Align the straight edge of a template along a short edge of the smaller rectangle. Trace the template and cut along the resulting outline. Set the cutout aside; then align and glue the remaining portion of the smaller rectangle atop the 6" x 9" piece of construction paper. Return the cutout to its original position; then—keeping the straight edge aligned—flip the cutout and glue it in place.

Cathy Schafman—Gr. 1
Prairie Hill School
South Beloit, IL

Adorable Angels

These cheerful cherubs are fun to make and they create quite a heavenly display!

To make the wings:
1. Fold a 6" x 12" tagboard strip in half (to 6" x 6").
2. Start at one corner and cut a series of scallops diagonally across the tagboard to the opposite corner.
3. Unfold the tagboard and cut along the crease to create two wing cutouts.
4. Pull apart several cotton balls; then glue a covering of cotton atop each cutout.

To make the face:
1. Use a template to trace a six-inch circle on skin-tone construction paper; then cut out the circle.
2. Glue on construction-paper curls and facial features. Add details with crayons or markers.

To make the clothing:
1. Fold a 4" x 9" strip of construction paper in half (to 4" x 4 1/2").
2. Starting at the fold, trim to round the two bottom corners as shown.
3. Unfold and decorate the resulting collar as desired.
4. Glue several crepe-paper or tissue-paper streamers to the back and lower edge of the collar.

To assemble and complete the project:
1. Glue the face to the top of the collar.
2. Glue a cotton-covered wing to each side of the face and collar.
3. Bend and twist one end of a pipe cleaner to make a halo; then tape the opposite end of the pipe cleaner to the back of the project.

Doris Hautala—Gr. 3, Washington Elementary, Ely, MN

wings 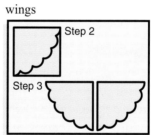 clothing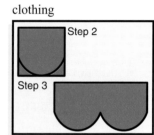

Trash-Bag Wreath

A wreath made out of trash bags? You saw it here first!

Materials For One Wreath:
1 wire coat hanger
7 white, plastic trash bags (13-gallon size), cut into 1" x 3" strips
scissors
1 decorative bow

1. Reshape the wire coat hanger into a circle.
2. Securely tie each strip onto the hanger and push it toward the top of the wreath. Continue in this manner until the hanger is full.
3. Trim any ragged edges from the wreath.
4. Attach a decorative bow to the top of the wreath.

Helen Rogers—Gr. 1, Siler City Elementary , Siler City, NC

Rudolph Replicas

Since Rudolph went down in history, there's a good chance these adorable reindeer necklaces will too!

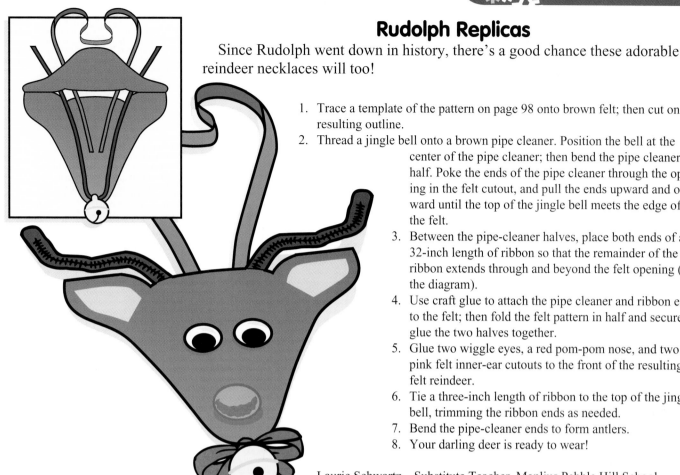

1. Trace a template of the pattern on page 98 onto brown felt; then cut on the resulting outline.
2. Thread a jingle bell onto a brown pipe cleaner. Position the bell at the center of the pipe cleaner; then bend the pipe cleaner in half. Poke the ends of the pipe cleaner through the opening in the felt cutout, and pull the ends upward and outward until the top of the jingle bell meets the edge of the felt.
3. Between the pipe-cleaner halves, place both ends of a 32-inch length of ribbon so that the remainder of the ribbon extends through and beyond the felt opening (see the diagram).
4. Use craft glue to attach the pipe cleaner and ribbon ends to the felt; then fold the felt pattern in half and securely glue the two halves together.
5. Glue two wiggle eyes, a red pom-pom nose, and two pink felt inner-ear cutouts to the front of the resulting felt reindeer.
6. Tie a three-inch length of ribbon to the top of the jingle bell, trimming the ribbon ends as needed.
7. Bend the pipe-cleaner ends to form antlers.
8. Your darling deer is ready to wear!

Laurie Schwartz—Substitute Teacher, Manlius Pebble Hill School
Dewitt, NY

Designs To Melt Your Heart

Round up a flat warming tray, waxed paper, broken crayons, and an adult volunteer, and you're ready to engage in the first step of this art experience! Set the warming tray on low. (Students complete the following procedure individually with adult supervision.) Lay a one-foot length of waxed paper on the surface of the tray. Melt part of a crayon on the paper by moving the tip of the crayon around on the warmed waxed paper. Repeat this process using several different colors. When the melted design is complete, place a second sheet of waxed paper on top of the melted crayon design; then remove the entire project from the tray.

When the projects have cooled, have students cut large seasonal shapes or patterns of smaller shapes (to create a stained-glass look) from 9" x 12" sheets of construction paper, then glue the papers atop the waxed paper designs. After students trim the excess waxed paper from the edges of their projects, tape the designs to a window for a remarkable holiday display.

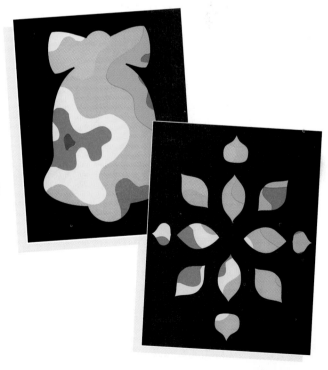

Stepping To The Beat

Rat-a-tat-tat! Since classic holiday stories bring to mind playthings from a simpler time, you'll find these stiff and stately geometric soldiers are a refreshing change of pace. To make a soldier, you will need a red 2-inch square (jacket); two red 3" x 1/2" strips (sleeves); a red 2" x 1 1/2" rectangle (hat); a tan, brown, or pink circle cut from a 1 1/2" square (face); a blue 6" x 2" rectangle (pants); a black 1" x 2" rectangle (shoes); a white 9" x 6" sheet of construction paper (background); some glue; markers; and gold glitter glue or a gold marking pen. To make a soldier from the geometric pieces, vertically place the blue rectangle on the background paper. Placing the black rectangle on the blue one, align it with the bottom and sides of the blue shape. Similarly place the red square on the blue rectangle, aligning it with the top and sides of the larger shape. Place the two long, narrow strips beside the other shapes to resemble the soldier's sleeves. Position the circle and the remaining rectangle so that they resemble a soldier's hat and face. Glue all of the pieces in place before embellishing them with markers and a gold pen or glitter glue to add the finishing touches to the soldier design. Rat-a-tat-tat! Rat-a-tat-tat! Rat-a-tat-tat!

Sr. M. Henrietta, Villa Sacred Heart, Danville, PA

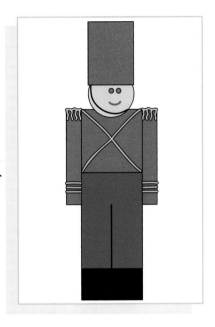

Dressed For The Holidays

Skip the mall—this student-made shirt is the perfect gift for classroom volunteers and other special adults.

Materials For One Shirt:

1 white sweatshirt
cardboard cut to fit inside the sweatshirt
green, yellow, and brown fabric paints
red and black, fine-tip fabric markers

scrap paper
pencil
1 plate

1. Insert the cardboard cutout inside the sweatshirt to prevent paint from bleeding through to the back of the shirt.
2. Using yellow fabric paint, paint a star at the top center of the shirt, just below the neckline.
3. On scrap paper, design a holiday thumbprint tree based on the number of students in your class. Using your design and a pencil, mark the shirt to indicate where each thumbprint should be.
4. Pour a small amount of green fabric paint onto a plate. Have each child press his thumb into the paint, then onto an indicated spot on the shirt.
5. To create the tree trunk, press your thumb into a small amount of brown fabric paint; then press it onto the shirt just below the last row of green prints.
6. When the paint dries, have each child add features to his thumbprint with a black, fine-tip fabric marker. Have him write his name next to his thumbprint with a red, fine-tip fabric marker. Add similar features to your brown thumbprint.

Cheryl Sergi—Gr. 2, Greene Central School, Greene, NY

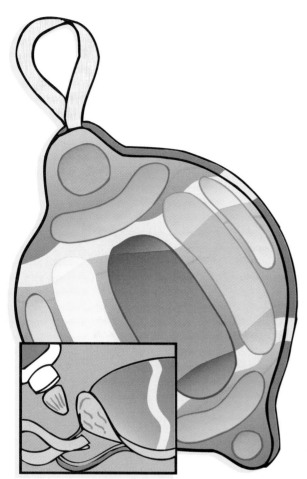

Dazzling Decorations

Dazzle your youngsters with this two-day holiday project. To make an ornament similar to the one shown, cut out a copy of the ornament pattern on page 99. Glue the resulting shape atop a slightly larger piece of tagboard or lightweight cardboard; then trim the cardboard to match the pattern. Working on newspaper, squeeze a thick trail of glue along each pattern line, including the outside cut lines. Allow the glue to dry overnight.

The following day lay the pattern—glue-side down—atop the dull side of a 5" x 7" piece of aluminum foil. Gently wrap the edges of the foil around the back of the pattern; then turn the pattern over and carefully press the foil into the ridges created by the hardened glue. Next trace the outline of the pattern on the dull side of a second piece of 5" x 7" foil. Cut out the resulting foil shape and glue it to the back of the pattern, leaving a small area at the top unattached. To make an ornament hanger, dab a bit of glue on each end of a two-inch length of ribbon. Press the ends of the ribbon into the foil opening; then glue the opening shut. Lastly use permanent markers to color the flat areas between the foil ridges.

Jeanne Knape, Davenport, IA

Stained-Glass Angel

Create a heavenly display with these colorful cherubs. Prepare a tagboard tracer of each of the patterns on page 100. Trace the larger pattern onto black construction paper and cut it out. Trace the two remaining patterns onto light blue, yellow, or pink construction paper and cut them out. Glue the two smaller cutouts atop the larger cutout as shown. Next align light blue, yellow, and pink strips of construction paper and hold them in one hand. Cut the strips to create a pile of triangular pieces. Carefully position the pieces atop the project so that small amounts of black can be seen between them, resulting in a stained-glass look. Glue the pieces in place. Spectacular!

Vida Vaitkus—Gr. 3
Marvin School
Stratford, CT

Festive Wreath

Spruce up your classroom for the holidays with wrapping-paper wreaths. In a parent note, request that each youngster bring to school several scraps of holiday gift wrap and one large bow. You will also need one paper plate and three red pom-poms per student. To make a wreath, cut the center out of a paper plate. Using a tagboard tracer, trace and cut out 15 to 20 holly leaves (patterns on page 99) from gift wrap. Glue the cutouts around the rim of the plate. When the rim is covered with "greenery," glue on three red pom-poms for berries. Add a bow as a cheery finishing touch.

Jeri Daugherity—Gr. 1
Mother Seton School
Emmitsburg, MD

Rudolph Puzzle Pins

It's no puzzle that these student-made pins will be a holiday hit! To make a pin, arrange three puzzle pieces to form a reindeer's head and antlers. Secure the pieces together using craft glue or a hot glue gun. When the glue is dry, paint the front, the back, and the sides of the project brown. (For best results use an acrylic paint.) Attach two wiggly eyes with craft glue. Then, using red and green puffy-paint pens, draw a red nose, green holly leaves, and red holly berries on the pin (see the illustration). When the project is dry, attach a pin back with hot glue. Wow! Rudolph never looked so good!

Ellen Meadors—Gr. 2
Rockbridge Elementary School
Stone Mountain, GA

A One-Of-A-Kind Ornament
Layers of fun for everyone!

Materials For One Ornament:
three 9" x 12" sheets of construction paper—each a different color
one 3" circle (or other simple holiday shape) template

pencil	1 heavy book	clear acrylic spray
glue	sand paper	1 paper clip
paintbrush	scissors	hot glue gun
waxed paper	glitter	one 5" length of ribbon

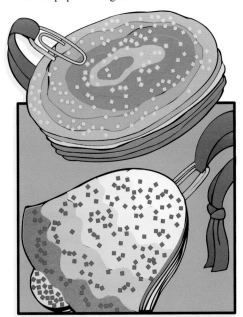

1. Trace the template onto each piece of construction paper six times. Cut out the shapes.
2. Making sure to cover the entire surface, paint a thin layer of glue on one side of one cutout; then align and press a second cutout of a different color atop the glue. Paint a thin layer of glue atop the newly placed cutout; then align and press a third cutout of a different color atop the glue. Repeat this process of painting and pressing until you have joined all of the cutouts.
3. Place the resulting ornament between two sheets of waxed paper. Set the heavy book on top of the project and allow the project to dry overnight.
4. Using a piece of sandpaper, sand both sides of the ornament. By sanding to various depths, you can achieve a wide variance in color. Continue rubbing until you have a desired design on each side of the ornament.
5. Paint a thin layer of glue over the entire surface of the ornament; then sprinkle the ornament with glitter.
6. In an open area, spray a coat of clear acrylic on the ornament. Allow drying time.
7. Use a hot glue gun to attach a paper clip to one side of the ornament.
8. Thread the ribbon through the paper clip. Tie the ribbon's ends.

Hope H. Taylor, Omaha, NE

Kwanzaa Trees

These colorful trees remind students and on-lookers that Kwanzaa celebrates family *and* seven important principles. To make a Kwanzaa tree, trace the outline of your hand (fingers outstretched) onto red paper seven times. Cut along the resulting outlines; then label each cutout with a different Kwanzaa principle, its meaning, and the day on which it is celebrated. Glue a 3" x 4" black rectangle to the bottom edge of a 12" x 18" sheet of green construction paper; then glue each of the seven hand cutouts to the paper to resemble tree foliage. Use a green glitter pen to add desired details. Cut the green paper away from the tree trunk and shape the tree to your liking. Mount the completed projects with the title "Kwanzaa Is A Time For Family And Growth!"

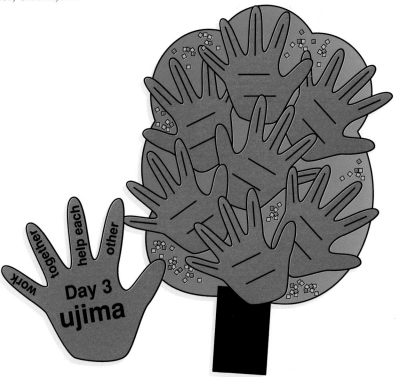

work together help each other
Day 3
ujima

First-Fruits Necklace

Kwanzaa is the African-American holiday reminiscent of traditional African harvests. Since the word Kwanzaa comes from a Swahili term meaning "first fruits," celebrate Kwanzaa this year by making first-fruits necklaces. To make a necklace, cut out three different fruit shapes from red construction paper and three more from green construction paper. From black paper, cut out the shape of Africa. Punch a hole near the tops of all seven shapes. If necessary, refer to a book such as *Kwanzaa* by Dorothy Rhodes Freeman and Dianne M. MacMillan (Enslow Publishers, Inc.) for the African terms, their translations, and the sequence in which they are introduced. Then write one of the principles of Kwanzaa and its translation on each of the seven shapes, putting the African term on one side and its translation on the other. (Since the first principle goes on the black cutout of Africa, either write the first principle and its translation with a white crayon or write them on small pieces of white paper and glue them on.) Tape the ends of a length of thick, black yarn to prevent raveling. Then, in the order shown, thread the labeled shapes onto the yarn along with red, green, and black beads or dyed pasta. Tie the ends of the yarn together, and wear the first-fruits necklace with pride.

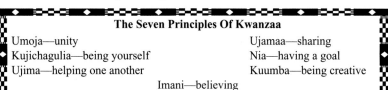

The Seven Principles Of Kwanzaa

Umoja—unity
Kujichagulia—being yourself
Ujima—helping one another

Ujamaa—sharing
Nia—having a goal
Kuumba—being creative

Imani—believing

Kwanzaa Candles

With paper loops and glue, students can create a festive *kinara* (candleholder) and the *mishumaa saba* (seven candles) that are traditionally lit during the seven-day Kwanzaa celebration.

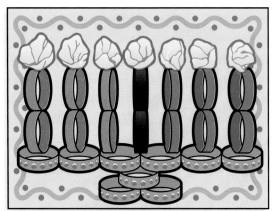

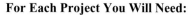

For Each Project You Will Need:
one 9" x 12" sheet of construction paper
nine 3/4" x 6" strips of brown construction paper
two 3/4" x 6" strips of black construction paper
six 3/4" x 6" strips of red construction paper
six 3/4" x 6" strips of green construction paper
seven 1 3/4" squares of yellow tissue paper
glue
pencil
markers, crayons, or colored glue

1. For each of the 23 strips, glue one end atop the other end to form a loop.
2. To make the candleholder, center and glue two brown loops horizontally at the bottom edge of the construction paper. Center and glue another brown loop above the first two. Then glue six brown loops in a row above the single loop.
3. To make each candle, glue two same-colored loops vertically atop the candleholder. Center the black candle, then glue three red candles to the left of it, and three green candles to the right of it.
4. To make a flame atop each candle, wrap a tissue-paper square around the eraser end of a pencil, dip it in glue, and press the tissue paper in position.
5. Add desired details to the project using markers, crayons, or colored glue.

Classy Calendar

Make the new year special with these personalized calendars.

Materials For One Calendar:
1 duplicated calendar page for each month of the year
1 duplicated calendar cover
student snapshots
1 plastic binding ring or individual rings for binding
hole puncher
various craft supplies and colors of construction paper
scissors
glue

1. Using blank calendar pages or a computer program that creates calendars, program a calendar page for each month of the year and a calendar cover. Indicate important information such as school holidays and students' birthdays on the calendar pages.
2. On heavy paper, duplicate a 12-month set of calendar pages.
3. Create a border of students' snapshots around the calendar cover; then duplicate a class set on heavy paper.
4. Distribute the pages and covers. Have each child sequence his calendar, then embellish and personalize his calendar cover as desired.
5. Bind each calendar using a plastic comb binding system. Or hole-punch the pages and use individual rings.
6. Using colorful construction paper and a variety of craft supplies, have students create an illustration or design for each month of the year and glue their projects inside their calendars. (Each project should be glued to the back of the page that precedes the month for which it was designed.)
7. To prepare the calendars for hanging, have each child hole punch the bottom center of each of his calendar pages.

Jane Williams—Gr. 1, Milan Elementary, Bluewater, NM

Dr. King Mobile

Keep Dr. Martin Luther King's dream alive with these patriotic mobiles. To make a mobile, glue a 5 1/2-inch, red construction-paper circle in the center of a 9-inch white paper plate. Color and cut out a copy of the Dr. King pattern on page 102; then glue the cutout in the center of the red circle. Use a blue marker or crayon to outline the rim of the plate as shown and to draw a large cloud shape on a 9" x 12" sheet of white construction paper. Cut out the cloud shape; then write a dream(s) for our world inside the shape. Hole-punch two holes in the top and bottom of the paper-plate project and in the top of the cloud shape. Thread a 12-inch length of red yarn through the holes at the top of the plate and tie the yarn ends. To connect the cloud cutout to the paper plate, thread a 12-inch length of red yarn through the remaining holes; then tie the yarn ends.

Barbara S. Johnson—Gr. 1, Greensboro Primary School, Greensboro, GA

My Dream
I dream that all children
will have peace.
I dream that everyone will have
clean water and enough food.
by Sarah

Freedom Bell

Martin Luther King, Jr., proclaimed that freedom rings throughout the country. These colorful bells are a wonderful reminder of Dr. King's wishes. To make a freedom bell, put dollops of red and white tempera paint on a disposable plate. Partially inflate a small balloon to a size that allows it to be held in one hand. Gently press the balloon into the paint; then press the painted balloon surface onto a 9" x 12" sheet of blue construction paper. For a feathery effect, slightly roll the balloon. Paint the surface of the blue paper using the manner described. When the painted paper has dried, trace a bell-shaped template onto the paper and cut along the resulting outline. Hole-punch the top and the bottom of the painted bell shape. On the blank side of the cutout, write a sentence that describes freedom. Thread a jingle bell onto a length of yarn and tie the yarn ends; then attach the jingle bell through the bottom hole in the project. Through the top hole, thread lengths of red, white, and blue curling ribbon. Tie the ribbon lengths and curl the resulting ribbon ends for a festive look. Display clusters of these freedom bells where air currents will occasionally cause them to move. Let freedom ring!

painting technique by Lona Claire Uzueta—Grs. K–1
Play N Learn, Fairbanks, AK

Happy Chinese New Year!

Ring in the Chinese New Year with this impressive class-created dragon! In a large open area that has a washable floor, display a length of white bulletin-board paper. If you plan to have eight student groups working on the project, visually divide the length of paper into seven equal sections and label each one with a different numeral from one to seven. On another length of bulletin-board paper, sketch a large dragon head. Label this section "8." Assign a small group of students to paint each section. Provide the same colors of paint for each group and encourage student creativity. When the paint has dried, cut out the dragon head and trim one end of the long paper length to resemble a dragon tail. For added interest, make a wavy cut along each side of the resulting dragon body. Then glue the dragon head to the dragon body. Display the impressive project in a school hallway. To add a 3-D effect, incorporate a few bends in the dragon. Totally hot!

Phoebe Sharp—Gr. 1
Gillette School, Gillette, NJ

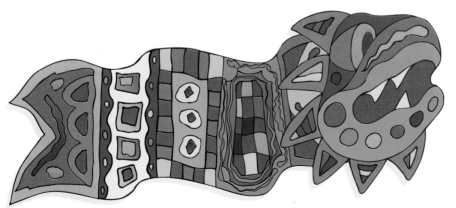

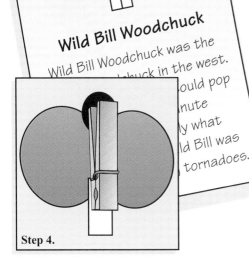

Wild Bill Woodchuck

Wild Bill Woodchuck was the
~~~~~~~~~huck in the west.
~~~~~~~~~ould pop
~~~~~~~~~nute
~~~~~~~~~y what
~~~~~~~~~ld Bill was
~~~~~~~~~ tornadoes.

Step 4.

A Furry Forecast

These wanna-be woodchucks are just in time for Groundhog Day!

For Each Woodchuck You Will Need:

— two 2" brown circles (ears)
— two 3 1/2" brown circles (cheeks)
— one 7" brown circle (head)
— two 1" pink circles (inner ears)
— one 1" x 2" white rectangle (teeth)
— two 1 1/2" white circles (eyes)
— one 1 1/2" black circle (nose)
— a black crayon or marker
— one wooden clothespin
— white glue
— craft glue
— scissors
— writing paper
— pencil

1. Glue each pink circle atop a 2-inch brown circle. Glue the resulting ears to the large brown circle (head). Set aside.
2. To make the cheeks, position the two 3 1/2-inch brown circles side by side so that they slightly overlap. Glue.
3. Glue the small black circle (nose) and the white rectangle (teeth) in place. Use the marker to add details to the teeth and cheeks.
4. Use craft glue to attach the clothespin to the back of the nose and teeth as shown. Allow drying time.
5. Position the cheeks atop the head; then use craft glue to secure the clothespin in the desired location. Allow drying time.
6. Pen a February forecast, a woodchuck-related tall tale, or another piece of creative writing; then clip your literary work in the woodchuck's mouth.

Laura Mihalenko—Gr. 2, Truman Elementary School, Parlin, NJ

Hearts Aplenty

Get to the heart of your youngsters' creativity with these one-of-a-kind valentine decorations! To begin, use a template to trace four heart shapes on red paper. Cut out each shape. To decorate the hearts, cut four designs from white paper, and glue each design to a different heart. When the glue has dried, fold each heart shape in half, keeping the design to the inside.

To assemble the project, place one folded heart in front of you. Spread glue on the top surface; then align a second folded heart atop the glue. In the same manner, glue the third heart to the second heart, and the fourth heart to the third heart. Then pick up the project, and glue the top and bottom surfaces together. Punch a hole near the top of the project. Thread one end of a length of curling ribbon through the hole and securely tie. Suspend this heartfelt example of creativity for all to see!

Lacy Valentines

Pretty-as-can-be valentines are just a heartbeat away using these easy-to-follow steps.

Materials For One Valentine:
iron, set on low
two 1' lengths of aluminum foil
handheld pencil sharpener
four crayons with their wrappers removed
one 8" heart template
one 8" square of white construction paper
one 10" square of white construction paper
one 9" square of colored construction paper
scissors
glue
hole puncher
pushpin

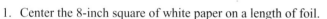

1. Center the 8-inch square of white paper on a length of foil.
2. Sharpen the crayons and spread the crayon shavings over the white paper.
3. Place the remaining length of foil on top of the crayon shavings.
4. Gently iron the top sheet of foil; then carefully remove it. (This step must be supervised [or completed] by an adult.)
5. When the crayon has hardened, trace a heart shape on the decorated paper.
6. Cut out the heart shape and glue it in the center of the colored paper.
7. Trim the colored paper to create a heart-shaped border.
8. Glue the project in the center of the 10-inch white square.
9. Trim the white paper to create an irregular heart-shaped border.
10. Use the hole puncher and the pushpin to give the white border a lacy look.
11. Write a desired valentine message on the back of the project.

Heart To Heart

These valentine keepsakes will surely help youngsters win the hearts of those they love. To make a heart-shape wreath, mix 1/4 cup of school glue with one teaspoon of water; then add 3/4 cup of mixed dried beans. Mold the bean mixture into the shape of a heart on a sheet of waxed paper. When the glue has completely dried, remove the heart-shaped wreath from the waxed paper and spray it with clear acrylic spray. Embellish the completed bean wreath with a ribbon bow.

Tami Fedor—Gr. 1, Lenoir City Elementary, Lenoir City, TN

template

Hearts Aflutter

These wings of love are just a heartbeat away! To make a butterfly, fold in half a 12" x 18" sheet of red, pink, or purple construction paper. Unfold the paper. Working atop newspaper, place several dollops of white tempera paint on one half of the paper. Refold the paper and gently rub the top of the folded paper with your open palm. Unfold the paper. When the paint has dried, refold the paper. Using a template like the one shown, trace a large heart shape on the folded paper. Cut on the resulting outline and unfold the paper. Attach a construction-paper body and bent pipe-cleaner antennae. Now that's a flamboyant flyer!

Elizabeth McDonald, Lincoln Elementary, Wichita, KS

One-Of-A-Kind Valentine Holders

Anything goes with these unique valentine holders! To make the basic holder, cut two identical heart shapes from wallpaper. Align one cutout atop the other; then trim the top cutout to make a pocket. Keeping the cutouts aligned, use a hole puncher to punch evenly spaced holes around the edges. Lace a length of ribbon or yarn through the holes. When the lacing is complete, tie the loose ribbon or yarn ends into a bow. Provide a generous supply of arts-and-crafts materials and invite students to personalize their holders any way they like!

Rita Arnold—ILP Manager
Alden Hebron School
Woodstock, IL

Heartfelt Messages

These valentine messages will surely help youngsters win the hearts of those they love. Use a ten-inch heart-shaped template to trace two heart shapes on tagboard or heavy paper. Cut out the resulting shapes and set one aside. Center and trace a seven-inch heart template atop the remaining cutout. Sponge-paint the smaller heart and sprinkle glitter atop the wet paint. Using a contrasting color of paint, sponge-paint the heart-shaped border. When the paint has dried, hole-punch a series of evenly spaced holes (about one inch apart) around the edge of the painted heart. Lace a length of ribbon through the holes, starting at the top of the heart and finishing there too. Fashion a bow from the ribbon ends. To complete the greeting, write a personalized valentine message on the second heart-shaped cutout. Use a brad fastener to join the two hearts. Happy Valentine's Day!

Kimberly Faraci—Gr. 1
Public School 19
Brooklyn, NY

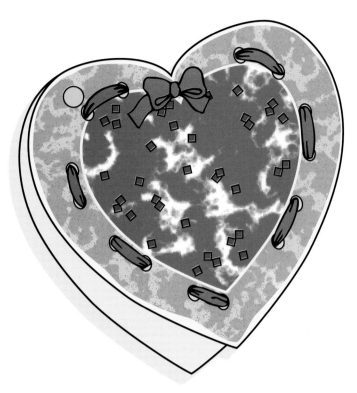

Haven Of Hearts

Why wait until spring to convert your classroom into a garden-like haven? Enlist the help of your youngsters in gathering a variety of papers and foils for cultivating these fancy flowers. To make a flower, cut out several heart shapes of various sizes from selected papers and/or foils. Decorate some of the cutouts using glitter glue pens, lace, and other craft supplies. Then arrange the heart cutouts into a flower blossom before gluing them in place. If desired, fold some of the hearts in half and glue sparingly along the folds so that the hearts retain a partially folded and dimensional effect. Attach a stem and leaves to complete the project. When the flower designs are dry, display them in clusters around your room.

Beth Jones—Grs. 1 & 2, General Vanier School
Niagara Falls, Ontario, Canada

Vivid Valentines

Pretty-as-can-be hearts are magically simple using this technique. Flatten a coffee filter. Fold the filter in half and cut a half-heart shape from it. Unfold the heart shape. Use watercolor markers to add some color to the cutout, intentionally leaving some spaces uncolored. Next place the heart on a stack of paper towels and use a spray bottle to lightly spray it with water. The colors will bleed randomly, creating interesting visual effects.

If desired, use a warm iron to press the heart cutout along with bits of tissue paper between two lengths of waxed paper. (Or use clear Con-Tact® covering.) Trim the waxed paper into a heart shape significantly larger than the filter heart. Use yarn or ribbon to suspend these translucent heart-shaped sparklers from the ceiling.

Lou Coakley—Gr. 3, Evans Elementary, Evans, GA

A Two-Heart Holder

Here's a valentine holder that's a cinch to make, and it has endless decorating possibilities. To begin, cut two same-size heart shapes from different colors of 12" x 18" construction paper. Fold each heart in half. Keeping the folds to the outside, bring the points of the hearts together and slip one folded heart just inside the other folded heart. Glue the overlapping edges, attach a paper handle, and personalize the resulting holder to your heart's desire!

Sharon Murphy
Greensboro, NC

Cupids 'n' Curls

These adorable cherubs are perfect for delivering your youngsters'
valentine wishes.

To make the wings:
1. Fold a 6" x 18" strip of pink construction paper
   in half (to 6" x 9").
2. Start at one corner and cut a series of scallops
   diagonally across the folded paper to the
   opposite corner.
3. Unfold and decorate the wings as desired.

To make the face:
1. Use a template to trace a five-inch circle on white construction
   paper.
2. Color the circle a desired skin tone; then cut it out.
3. Glue on construction-paper facial features and curling-ribbon hair.

To make the heart and hands:
1. Cut a heart shape from a 4 1/2" x 6" strip of red construction paper.
2. Fold in half a 3" x 6" strip of white construction paper.
3. Draw a chubby hand like the one shown on the folded paper and
   cut on the outline.
4. Color the cutouts a desired skin tone.

To assemble and complete the project:
1. Glue the face and heart to the wings.
2. Glue a hand on each side of the heart.
3. Write a valentine message on the heart.

Vicki Giermann
Laveen Elementary School
Laveen, AZ

General George

Create a visual salute to General George Washington
with this eye-catching project. To begin, trim the lower
corners of a 6" x 9" sheet of pink paper for George's face.
Fold an 8" x 6" sheet of white paper in half (to 4" x 6");
then cut an irregular shape through both thicknesses,
creating two identical hair pieces. For George's hat, fold a
4" x 12" piece of dark blue paper to 4" x 6". Trim the
unfolded end diagonally and cut a V-shaped notch as
shown. Unfold the paper and glue a narrow strip of
yellow paper to the hat cutout. Glue the face, hair, and hat
patterns together. Use paper scraps and crayons to
complete George's face and collar. By George, isn't that a
dapper guy?

Audrey M. Brenholt—Gr. 1, Roselawn Elementary, Chetek, WI

Presidents' Windsock

Herald the arrival of Presidents' Day with these bright and breezy windsocks!

Materials For One Windsock:
template of President Lincoln's profile (pattern, page 103)
template of President Washington's profile (pattern, page 103)
star-shaped template
one 12" x 18" sheet of blue construction paper
three 2" x 18" strips of red construction paper
one 9" x 12" sheet of black construction paper
one 9" x 12" sheet of white construction paper
four 16-inch strips of red crepe paper
four 16-inch strips of white crepe paper
one 36-inch length of yarn
pencil
glue
scissors
hole puncher

1. Glue the red paper strips to the blue paper as shown.
2. Trace each presidential profile on black paper.
3. Cut out and glue each profile to the project.
4. Trace several stars on the white paper.
5. Cut out and glue the stars to the project.
6. When the glue has dried, roll the blue paper into a cylinder (keeping the decorations to the outside) and glue the overlapping edges together.
7. Alternating colors, glue the crepe-paper strips inside the lower rim of the project.
8. At the top of the cylinder, punch two holes opposite each other.
9. Thread each end of the yarn length through a different hole and securely tie.

adapted from an idea by Doris Hautala—Gr. 3, Washington Elementary, Ely, MN

Famous Folks

Get to the heart of the matter with this presidential project. Duplicate the patterns on page 103 onto black construction paper; then cut out each presidential profile. Mount each cutout on a 6" x 8" white construction-paper rectangle. Stack the rectangles and trim the edges to create two equal-sized ovals. Mount each oval on a 7" x 9" rectangle of blue paper. Trim each blue rectangle to create an eye-catching border. Cut a large heart shape from a 12" x 18" sheet of red construction paper; then mount one project on each side of the heart cutout. Punch a hole near the top of the project and suspend it from the ceiling.

Judy Goodman, Perryville Elementary, Perryville, MO

Lions And Lambs

You've heard the old saying, "March comes in like a lion and goes out like a lamb." That makes March the perfect time to get *wild* and *woolly* with these adorable critters! To make a lion, color or sponge-paint a 6-inch paper plate yellow or light brown. Attach wiggle eyes and use a permanent marker to draw a nose and mouth. To make the lion's mane, begin with a supply of 6" x 1/2" brown paper strips. One at a time, wrap a paper strip around a pencil; then slide the strip off and glue it—standing on edge—to the rim of the plate. When the mane is completed, cut a pair of lion ears from brown paper and glue them in place.

To make a lamb, begin with a white 6-inch paper plate. Attach wiggle eyes, draw a nose and mouth, and fashion a woolly coat for the lamb using 6" x 1/2" white paper strips and the technique described above. Cut a pair of lamb ears from black paper and glue them in place. Showcase the furry friends on a bulletin board titled "Watching The Weather."

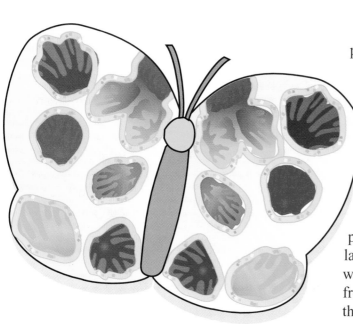

Breathtaking Butterflies

Colorful, intriguing, and unique—these butterfly impostors are sure to prompt plenty of oohs and aahs! Before you begin the project, pour each of several colors of tempera paint into individual empty glue (squeeze) bottles for easy dispensing. To make a butterfly, fold a 12" x 18" sheet of white construction paper in half; then unfold the paper and lay it on newspaper. Squeeze blobs of colorful paint on one half of the paper. Refold and carefully rub the paper to spread and transfer the paint inside; then open the paper. When the paint is dry, refold the paper. Starting at the fold and ending at the fold, cut out a large wing shape. Unfold the cutout to reveal a pair of wings. Fashion a body, a head, and a pair of antennae from construction paper. Glue the cutouts to the project; then use a permanent marker, glue and glitter, or a glitter pen to outline the colorful splotches on each wing. Now that's a fancy flyer!

Alice Arksey—Grs. 2–3
Northridge Public School
London, Ontario, Canada

Leprechaun Look-Alikes

Keep these adorable leprechauns around and you'll have the luck of the Irish at your fingertips!

Materials For One Leprechaun:

one 4 1/2" x 12" piece of green construction paper (body)
one 4" x 8" piece of green construction paper (hat)
one 2" x 8" piece of green construction paper (sleeves)
one 5" skin-tone construction-paper circle (head)
two 2" squares of skin-tone construction paper (hands)
one 2" x 4" piece of white construction paper (bow tie)

one 2" x 6" piece of orange construction paper (hair)
five 1' strips of orange crepe paper
markers or crayons
construction-paper scraps
scissors
glue

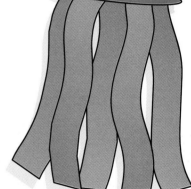

Steps:

1. **To make the body,** roll the 4 1/2" x 12" piece of green paper into a cylinder and glue it. Position the seam at the back and glue the top one inch of the cylinder closed. When dry, trim to round each glued corner.

2. **To make the sleeves and hands,** fold in half the 2" x 8" piece of green paper, cut out two matching sleeves, and glue them in place. Stack the skin-toned squares, cut out two matching hand shapes, and glue them in place.

3. **To make the hair, hat, and face,** snip the orange paper into several 1/2" x 2" lengths. Glue the resulting hair to the skin-toned circle. Fold the 4" x 8" piece of green paper in half (to a 4-inch square) and draw half of a hat shape on the paper as shown below. Cut on the outline; then unfold the cutout and add desired decorations. Glue the hat to the top of the circle. Add facial features and glue the resulting head to the top of the body.

4. **To make the bow tie,** buttons, and streamers, cut a bow-tie shape from the piece of white paper, decorate the shape as desired, and glue it in place. Cut out, decorate, and glue several buttons to the front of the body. Glue the crepe-paper strips in side the lower rim of the project.

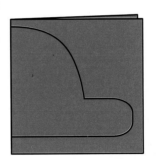

adapted from an idea by Doris Hautala—Gr. 3
Washington Elementary
Ely, MN

Recycled Wonders

Looking for a unique art medium? Look no further than your morning newspaper. Cut sections of newspapers into various shapes, attempting to locate some pieces with lots of black ink to contrast with others that have less ink. Fold, curl, accordion-fold, and bend the paper pieces to give some of the elements a three-dimensional effect. On black construction paper, arrange the pieces of newsprint to resemble a spring flower garden complete with butterflies. Add details sparingly with white and black paint pens or markers. Then glue the pieces in place. What's black and white and refreshingly unusual? This project!

Pond Life

Set the scene for this painting activity by reading aloud a pond-related book such as *In The Small, Small Pond* by Denise Fleming (Henry Holt And Company, Inc.; 1993) or *Pond Year* by Kathryn Lasky (Candlewick Press, 1997). Then, working atop a paper-covered surface, use diluted watercolors to paint a desired pond scene. When the project dries, outline the pond life shown with a black marker. Embellish the project with construction-paper details as desired. The results are "pond-itively" striking!

Joan M. Macey, Binghamton, NY

Beauteous Blooms

When these colorful flowers take center stage, heads will turn! Cut leftover scraps of construction paper into narrow strips (approximately 1/2" x 3"). One at a time, roll each of several paper strips around a pencil, slide the rolled paper off the pencil, and glue one end of the strip to a four-inch construction-paper circle. Continue in this manner until the entire surface of the circle is covered. For best results glue the paper strips close together. Then trim six 3" x 4" pieces of colorful construction paper to resemble petals. Glue the petals side by side around the back edge of the circle cutout. Glue a stem cut from green paper onto the back of the flower; then glue a desired number of leaf cutouts along the stem. Showcase the flowers side by side on a bulletin board or wall for an eye-catching garden display.

Doris Hautala—Gr. 3
Washington Elementary
Ely, MN

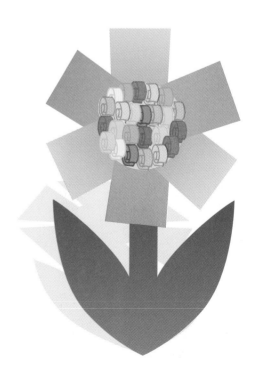

All Aflutter!

These eye-catching butterflies can be created in just a flit and a flutter! Invert a small-size disposable paper soup bowl; then use colorful tempera paints to paint the bottom of the bowl. While the paint is drying, trim four 4 1/2" x 6" sheets of construction paper to resemble butterfly wings and two 2" x 4" strips of black construction paper to resemble butterfly antennae. Arrange the wing and antennae cutouts so that they achieve the desired results when the inverted bowl is in place. Glue together all overlapping surfaces of the wing and antennae cutouts, creating one large shape. Squeeze a trail of glue around the rim of the bowl; then invert the bowl on the construction-paper shape. Gently press on the bowl until the glue dries. Now that's a colorful flier!

Doris Hautala—Gr. 3
Washington Elementary

Chasing Rainbows

Have each of your youngsters welcome spring by fashioning his own double-sided rainbow. To make a rainbow, you will need a rainbow-shaped template. Trace the pattern onto white paper twice, creating two separate rainbow shapes. Using tempera paints in assorted rainbow colors, create two matching rainbows by painting each shape the same. When the paint has dried, cut out the shapes and position the cutouts side by side, painted sides down. Glue several crepe-paper streamers to the ends of each rainbow; then flip over one cutout and align it atop the other so that the painted surfaces are to the outside. Staple the cutouts together, leaving a generous opening at the top; then carefully tuck a desired amount of crumpled newspaper strips in the opening. When the project is sufficiently stuffed, staple the opening closed. Pull apart several cotton balls (or use polyester batting) and glue fluffy clouds at the ends of the rainbow. Suspend the rainbow from monofilament line and watch it dance and twirl in the springtime breezes.

Kimberly Spring—Grs. 2 & 3, Lowell Elementary, Everett, WA

Bouncin' Blossoms

When these colorful flowers take center stage, thoughts of spring will surely start popping into everyone's mind. Using circle templates (provide several sizes), trace and cut out a desired number of construction-paper circles. Make a spiral cut to the center of each circle; then gently pull the resulting spiral upward, giving the cutout dimension. On an 11" x 17" sheet of construction paper, arrange the spiral-cut circles into a flower blossom. Secure the cutouts in place by gluing only the outer rim of each one to the larger paper. Add a construction-paper stem and leaves. Mount the completed project onto a 12" x 18" sheet of construction paper in a contrasting color. Encourage students to create flowers in a variety of shapes and sizes.

Sr. Ann Claire Rhoads
Baltimore, MD

Woven Pop Art

Recycle plastic six-pack rings into unique pieces of pop art! Cut a supply of construction- and wall-paper scraps into six-inch and ten-inch strips of varying widths. First weave the longer strips through the plastic rings; then weave the shorter strips through the plastic rings and the longer paper strips. When the weaving is complete, trim the ends of the paper strips to create a desired look. Glue the weaving to a 6" x 9" rectangle of construction paper that is mounted atop a slightly larger paper rectangle of a contrasting color. This earth-friendly project is perfect for an Earth Day celebration!

Melanie J. Miller
Nashport, OH

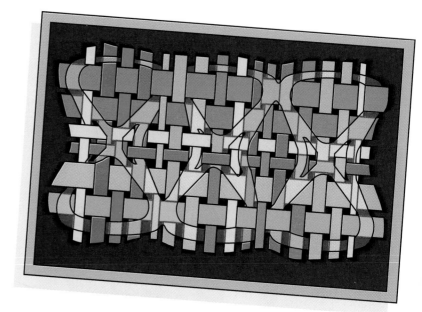

Spring

Extraordinary Eggs

Inspire uniquely decorated Easter eggs using this combination technique. To begin, trace an egg shape onto art paper. Inside the egg outline, randomly drip thinned tempera paint; then blow through a drinking straw to transform the paint drips into desired shapes. When the paint is completely dry, use a colored pencil in a contrasting color to completely fill each unpainted area within the egg outline. Cut out the egg shape. Display the egg and others like it on a seasonal bulletin board. Or mount the cutout on a slightly larger piece of contrasting construction paper and trim the construction paper to create a narrow border. The project can be used as a booklet cover for student work, or it can be hole-punched and suspended from a length of monofilament line. "Egg-ceptional"!

Mary Grace Ramos—Gr. 2
Pinewood Acres School
Miami, FL

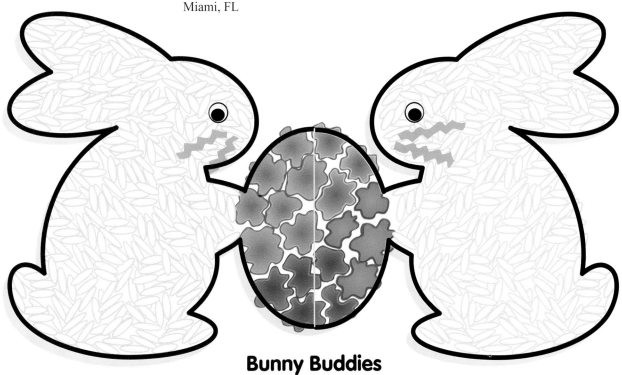

Bunny Buddies

Everyone will be hopping over to take a look at these furry-looking friends! Use the pattern on page 105 to create a template; then trace the template on tagboard and cut on the resulting outline. To decorate the egg, use colorful tissue-paper squares and the following method: Center the eraser end of a pencil over a small square of tissue paper. Wrap the paper upward around the pencil. Holding the paper in place, dip it in glue and press it onto the desired location. When the egg is decorated, attach a wiggle eye and add a coat of uncooked rice to each bunny. To do this, use a glue-soaked piece of sponge with a clipped-on clothespin handle to apply a coat of glue to each bunny shape. Attach wiggle eyes; then evenly sprinkle rice over the glued area until the bunny shapes are completely covered. If desired, carefully press paper whiskers in place. When the glue has dried, lift the project, tap off any excess rice, and display the bunny buddies for all to admire. Hop to it!

Rita Arnold—ILP Manager, Alden Hebron Grade School, Hebron, IL

Springtime Baskets

These colorful woven baskets are perfect for delivering springtime, Easter, or May Day surprises! To make a basket, use a ruler and a pencil to divide a 9" x 12" sheet of construction paper into nine 1" x 12" strips. Cut out the strips and lay two aside. Arrange the seven remaining strips side by side; then tape down each end along one edge. Next cut a 9" x 12" sheet of contrasting construction paper into 1" x 12" strips as described above. Set two strips aside, and weave the remaining seven strips in and out of the first set of seven. To assemble the basket, slide the woven strips toward the center of the project; then—one side at a time—gather and staple together the ends of the strips. Use two of the extra strips for handles, stapling them to the basket as shown. How pretty!

Mary E. Morgan—Gr. 1
South Roxana Elementary
South Roxana, IL

Bunny Cups

Hippity, hoppity! Top off your Easter festivities by tucking a few treats into these student-made bunny cups. Start with a Styrofoam® cup or cover a colored disposable cup with white art paper. Attach construction-paper ears, eyes, and whiskers; then secure a pink pom-pom nose in place. Tuck some cellophane grass inside the decorated cup, and it's ready for treats. Everyone will be hopping over to see what these adorable bunnies have delivered!

Sponge-Painted Bunnies

These adorable bunnies will capture your heart! Using pastel shades of paint, sponge-paint a 12" x 18" sheet of white construction paper. When the paint is dry, use tagboard templates to trace a ten-inch and a seven-inch heart shape on the paper. Cut out the two shapes. Glue the rounded end of the smaller heart (the head) atop the point of the larger heart (the body). Cut bunny ears from two 2" x 6" strips of construction paper. Cut two inner-ear shapes from your painted scraps. Mount each inner-ear cutout atop an ear cutout; then glue the completed ears in place. Attach construction-paper facial features and a crepe-paper bow. Use crayons or markers to draw other desired details. Look who's ready to hop down the bunny trail!

Carol Nelson—Gr. 2
C. C. Lee School
Aberdeen, SD

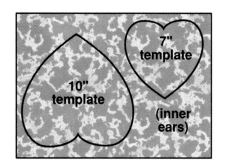

Peep! Peep!

You probably won't hear a peep out of your youngsters while they're busy crafting these spring chicks. To make a construction-paper chick, trace both hands and one large egg-shaped template on yellow paper. Cut out the resulting shapes. For movable wings, use brads to attach the hand cutouts as shown. Gently pull forward the finger and thumb portions of each hand cutout to add dimension. Cut two large eyes from white paper. Add pupils using a marker; then glue the eyes in place. For the chick's beak, fold an orange-paper square in half diagonally and glue it on. Also attach two orange-paper feet. Now that's an art project that's all it's clucked up to be!

Connie Carver—Gr. 1
St. Charles School
Parma, OH

59

A Funny Bunny

Hippity hoppity! Look what's headed your way—a "weally" whimsical "wabbit" that's up to some bunny business!

For each bunny you will need:
9" x 12" sheet of white construction paper (body)
two 3" x 12" pieces of white construction paper (ears and arms)
2" x 9" piece of pink construction paper (inner ears)
3" x 6" piece of white construction paper (feet)
2" x 2" piece of pink construction paper (nose)
2" x 4" piece of black construction paper (whiskers)
4" x 5" piece of yellow construction paper (basket)
scraps of colorful construction paper for egg basket
scissors
glue
crayons or markers

Directions:

1. **For the bunny's body,** roll the 9" x 12" sheet of white paper into a cylinder and glue it. Position the seam at the back of the project; then glue the top one inch of the cylinder closed. When the glue dries, trim to round each of the glued corners.

2. **For the bunny's ears,** fold in half one 3" x 12" piece of white paper and cut out two matching ear shapes. Fold in half the 2" x 9" piece of pink paper and cut out two matching inner-ear shapes. Glue one pink cutout inside each white cutout. Glue the resulting ears to the body.

3. **For the bunny's arms,** fold in half the remaining 3" x 12" piece of white paper and cut out two matching arm shapes. Glue the arms to the body.

4. **For the bunny's feet,** fold in half the 3" x 6" piece of white paper and cut out two matching feet shapes (see the illustration). Add desired details; then glue the feet to the body.

5. **For the bunny's face,** fold in half the 2" x 2" piece of pink paper and cut out a heart shape. Cut the 2" x 4" strip of black paper into narrow strips. Glue the resulting whiskers to the nose; then glue the nose to the body. Attach eyes made from construction-paper scraps, or draw them using crayons or markers.

6. **To make the basket,** fold the yellow paper in half and cut out a basket shape (see the illustration). Cut out construction-paper grass and eggs; then glue them in the basket. Slip the basket onto the bunny's arm.

Step 4

Step 6

An Expression Of Love

The love that fills this Mother's Day greeting keeps growing and growing and growing!

For each card you will need:

6" x 18" piece of construction paper (card)
3 1/2" x 5" piece of construction paper (flowerpot)
four 3" x 3" pieces of colorful construction paper (flowers)
1/2" x 12" piece of green construction paper (plant stem)

scraps of colorful construction paper for leaves and
   flower centers
scissors
crayons
glue

Directions:

1. To make the flowerpot, fold and trim the 3 1/2" x 5" piece of construction paper as shown. Glue the cutout at the lower edge of the card.

2. Glue the green-paper stem to the card, tucking one end of the stem just below the surface of the flowerpot. Allow to dry.

3. Cut a flower shape from each 3" x 3" piece of paper. Decorate each flower shape as desired. Set aside.

4. Bend the top of the card forward until it is flush with the top of the flowerpot. Hold the paper in place; then flatten and fold it.

5. Repeat step 4, this time bringing the fold to the top of the flowerpot.

6. Unfold the card. Starting at the top, fold the card forward at each crease.

7. With the card folded, glue a flower cutout above the flowerpot. In the top left-hand corner, use a crayon to write "My Love For You." In the lower right-hand corner of the folded paper, write "Just Grows,". Then unfold one section at a time and glue a flower on the folded paper above the stem. Each time write "And Grows," in the lower right-hand corner of the folded paper. When the card is completely unfolded, write "And Grows!" to the right of the flower. Add desired leaves to the stem.

8. Use a crayon to write "Happy Mother's Day!", the date, and your name on the flowerpot. Then refold the project to proudly present it to Mom!

Louis Lessor—Gr. 2
Westside Elementary
Sun Prairie, WI

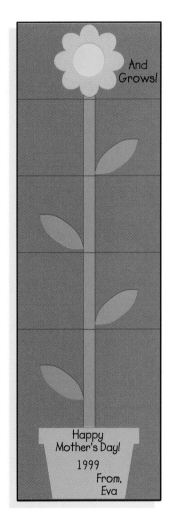

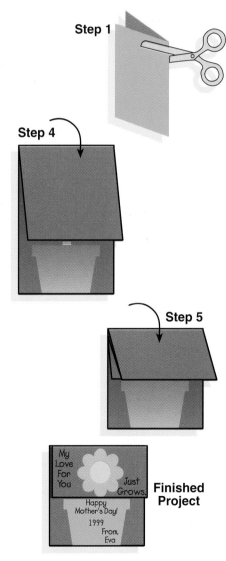

Nifty Necklaces

Youngsters can fashion these one-of-a-kind necklaces for Mother's Day gifts or for another gift-giving occasion. Working atop waxed paper, roll out an individual portion of self-hardening clay to a thickness of approximately one-quarter inch. Use a cookie cutter or a stencil and a plastic knife to cut a desired shape from the clay. Engrave desired details with a toothpick or another similar object; then use a drinking straw to cut two holes in the cutout for hanging. Allow the clay to completely harden, turning it occasionally. Add touches of color to the hardened clay with acrylic paint before sealing the artwork with a light coat of clear enamel. Finally thread the artwork onto a 32-inch length of ribbon or macramé cord. Tie the ribbon or cord ends, and the necklace is ready to wear!

Janette Anderson—Gr. 1
James Leitch Elementary
Fremont, CA

Marvelous Mother's Day Magnets

Each of your children can present a bouquet of long-lasting posies to his mom for Mother's Day. To make a few small flower-shaped magnets, mix plaster of paris according to package directions. Pour the mixture into flower-shaped candy molds. When the plaster is dry, remove the flower shapes from the mold. Use tempera paint and a small brush to paint each shape. Allow the paint to dry completely; then spray the shapes with acrylic spray. When the acrylic coating is dry, attach a magnet strip to the back of each shape. Voila! These perfectly delightful posies will definitely make Mom's day!

Deborah Howard—Gr. 3
Bellows Free Academy
Fairfax, VT

Hats Off To Moms

Are you "brimming" with great ideas for how to tell mom she's head and shoulders above the rest? Try this!

Materials For One Hat:
1 paper plate
1 pencil
one 9" x 12" piece of floral-print wallpaper
three 9" x 12" sheets of white construction paper
scissors or pinking shears
glue
1 paintbrush
1 unopened can or lidded jar with a 3" diameter
one 12" length of wide ribbon
1 paper clip
hot glue gun
one 9" length of narrow ribbon

1. Using the paper plate as a template, trace a circle on the wallpaper and each of the three sheets of white construction paper. Cut out the resulting circles.
2. Making sure to cover the entire surface, paint a thin layer of glue on one side of one construction-paper circle. Align and press a second construction-paper circle atop the glue. Paint a thin layer of glue atop the newly placed circle, and align and press the remaining construction-paper circle in place. Repeat the gluing process; then align and press the wallpaper circle atop the glue.
3. With the wallpaper circle on top, center the stack of cutouts over the can. Form the hat's crown and brim by shaping the project over the end of the can. Leave the project in place and allow it to dry.
4. Fashion a bow from the wide ribbon and glue it to the hat as shown.
5. Use a hot glue gun to attach the paper clip beneath the hat rim—opposite the bow.
6. Thread the narrow ribbon through the paper clip. Tie the ribbon's ends and suspend the project in a desired location.

Joan M. Macey, Binghamton, NY

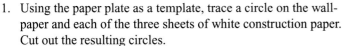

Colorful Collectables

With a little creativity, it's easy to dish up this keepsake gift. Using permanent markers, decorate the face of a white plastic Rubbermaid® dinner plate (available at most department stores). Also sign and date the back of the plate. To seal the artwork, spray the face of the plate with a light coat of clear enamel. There you have it—a decorative plate to brighten Mom's kitchen.

Alice Elaine Fink—Gr. 3
Krebs Public School
Krebs, OK

Coffee-Filter Corsages

Here's a pretty, decorative corsage for a very special lady. Use colorful markers to embellish each of five paper coffee filters. Be creative—anything goes! Coloring a solid band around the rim of each filter adds a nice touch. Stack the decorated filters; then pinch together the bottoms as shown. Bend a five-inch length of green pipe cleaner in half. Slip the pinched portion of the filters between the open ends of the pipe cleaner. Tightly wrap a length of masking or floral tape around the pinched filters, securing the pipe cleaner in place. Carefully pull the coffee filters apart to open the flower. Someone is going to feel very proud to have this corsage pinned to her clothing!

Luddie Johnson
Lake Primary School
St. Amant, LA

Mom's Fan

What mom wouldn't be pleased to receive a pretty decorative fan from her biggest fan—her youngster? To make a fan, begin by accordion-folding a ten-inch square of wallpaper. (More advanced youngsters may glue lace around the perimeter of the wallpaper backing before folding.) Staple the folded wallpaper about one-third of the way up. Fan out both the upper and the lower sections of paper. Glue or staple the sides of the fan together as shown. Attach a ribbon loop to the back of the fan for hanging. Glue a small bow and perhaps a few sprigs of baby's breath on the front of the fan. It's a "fan-tastic" gift!

Donna Fischer—Gr. 3
Holy Rosary School
St. Marys, OH

A Sewing Kit For Mom

Moms will be "sew" pleased when they receive this practical and pretty Mother's Day gift. To make a sewing kit that will fit nicely into a purse, cut a 5" x 8" unlined index card in half, creating two 2 1/2" x 8" strips. (Set one strip aside for a second kit, if desired.) Use a scissors blade to score the strip about an inch from one end and 3 1/4" from the other end. (You may want to do this for the youngsters before giving them the index-card halves.) Then turn the strip over and fold the ends forward, bending the strip at the scoring marks to create a cover that resembles a matchbook cover. Color and personalize the sewing kit cover as desired. For a card to hold thread, use scissors to cut three pairs of diagonal slits in the sides of a 2" x 3" piece of tagboard or index card. Wrap three different colors of thread around the card, securing each color of thread in a pair of slits. To hold a few sewing needles, cut a 2" x 3" piece of fabric with pinking shears. Staple the fabric and the thread card inside the folded cover; then insert needles in the fabric to complete the kit.

Phyllis Kidder
Edward C. Killin Elementary School
Okinawa, Japan

Poetic Planter

A flower and a rhyme—what more could a mother ask for?

Materials For One Planter:
blank paper
1 pencil
1 arc-shaped construction- paper pattern (page 102)
fine-tipped markers
scissors
two 9-oz. clear plastic cups

clear tape
craft glue
1 spoon
1 cup potting soil
1 seedling
water

Steps:
1. Write a poem on the blank paper. (Use the writing suggestions provided with the pattern on page 102.)
2. Use markers to copy and decorate your poem on the arc-shaped pattern.
3. Cut out the pattern.
4. Wrap the cutout around the outside of one plastic cup so that it is approximately 1/4 inch from the cup bottom. Tape the ends of the cutout together.
5. Dab glue around the bottom rim of the cup; then securely set the cup inside the second cup.
6. Spoon the potting soil into the cup.
7. Plant the seedling in the soil; then sprinkle the soil with water.

Linda C. Buerklin—Substitute Teacher
Monroe Township, Williamstown, NJ

Bask In The Glow

It's the time of year when everyone welcomes the warmth of the sun. Why not bring a bright-and-cozy aura into your classroom by having each student make a paper-plate sun? To make a sun, visualize an imaginative personified design and sketch it onto a paper plate. Then use crayons, markers, or tempera paints to "colorize" the design. To give your design radiant shine and sparkle, consider adding colored glues and clear glitter. Grab your shades! Here comes the sun!

Marsha Black & Michelle McAuliffe
Greensburg, IN

Showy Sunflowers

Big and bold, these striking sunflower projects create a stunning display! Begin by cutting a six-inch circle from white construction paper. Using brown tempera paint, sponge-paint the resulting cutout and set it aside. Trace and cut out approximately 30 petal shapes from yellow paper. (If desired, use the patterns on page 107 to create tagboard templates for this purpose.) Glue a row of petals side by side around the back edge of the circle cutout. Glue a second row of petals behind the first, so that their tips can be seen between the existing row. Repeat a third time. To give the project dimension, fold some of the petals forward. Glue a long stem cut from green paper onto the back of the flower; then glue a desired number of leaf cutouts along the stem. Showcase the giant flowers side by side on a bulletin board or wall for an eye-catching garden display.

Rita Andreu—Gr. 3
Sabal Palm Elementary
Ponte Vedra, FL

Flashy Fireflies

You'll attract lots of attention with a display of these flashy fireflies. To make the beetle's body, trim to round the corners of a 2" x 7" strip of green construction paper. Use a green crayon or marker to divide the body into three sections: the head, the thorax, and the abdomen. Cut a small notch in the rounded end of the head; then color and round the resulting eyes as desired. Cut a wing from each of two 3" x 4 1/2" strips of yellow paper and each of two 3" x 3 1/2" pieces of waxed paper. Glue the narrow ends of the yellow wings to the firefly's thorax; then glue the narrow ends of the waxed-paper wings to the yellow wings. To complete the bug, glue clear sequins or glitter to the end of its abdomen. Mount the completed projects on a bulletin board covered with black paper. For added appeal, use sturdy tape to attach a strand of clear Christmas-tree lights to the display. Periodically, under close supervision, illuminate the lights for a breathtaking display!

Michele Baerns—Gr. 2
Sevierville Primary School, Sevierville, TN

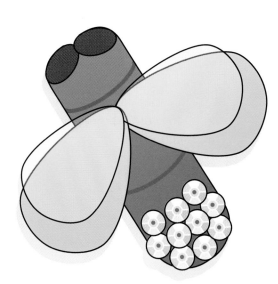

Fun Suncatchers

Catch your student's attention with these fun suncatchers. Then let the sunshine in!

one 4 1/2" x 9" piece of clear Con-Tact® covering
flowers and/or leaves that have been picked, dried, and
  flattened by the student
8 craft sticks
craft glue
one 9" length of string or fishing line
scissors

1. Fold the Con-Tact® covering in half and crease it. Unfold.
2. Lay the covering on a flat surface, backing-side up; then peel away the backing.
3. In the center of one half of the covering, arrange the dried items.
4. Fold the remaining half of the covering over the dried items, aligning the edges. Set aside.
5. Use four craft sticks to make a frame. To do this, arrange two sticks parallel to each other and about 4 1/2 inches apart. Place the two remaining sticks on top of—and perpendicular to—the other two sticks. Glue the sticks in place. Allow to dry.
6. To make a second frame, repeat step 5. Before gluing the sticks in place, loop and tie the length of string around one stick. This will be your hanger.
7. Glue the dried arrangement on top of the first frame. When the glue has dried, trim away any covering that extends beyond the frame.
8. Glue the second frame on top of the project, keeping the hanger free from glue.
9. To display the project, turn it diagonally and slide the hanger to one corner. Suspend the project in a sunny window.

Mary Lam Boardwine—Library Media Specialist
Montvale Elementary School, Montvale, VA

Of all the dads
In the deep blue sea,
I'm so glad
You're the one for me!

Jason

Buckets Of Fun

As summertime gift-giving occasions approach, stock up on empty frosting tubs or other cylindrical containers. You will also need at least one small fish-shaped sponge. To convert a container into a work of art, first examine the container you'll be using. If it has artwork and wording that you will need to cover, wrap the container with construction paper cut to fit it. If the container is already a solid color, it's ready for decoration. Dip a fish-shaped sponge in colored glue, blot the sponge, and press it onto the side of the container. Repeat these steps to add additional fish and other sea creatures to the container and also to a square of paper cut to fit inside the container. Further embellish the container, as desired. When the glue has dried, write a message on the square for the gift's recipient. Punch or poke two holes opposite one another near the rim of the container. Hook the ends of two intertwined pipe cleaners into the holes to make a bucket handle. Then place the message square inside the bucket along with a plastic bag of Gummy Worm® candies or fish-shaped crackers. Won't someone be surprised!

Kirsten Willer—Grs. 2 & 3
Trinity Lutheran School, West Allis, WI

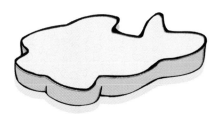

Magnetic Note Holder

Here's a gift-giving idea that's perfect for Father's Day! Use the hammer pattern on page 108 to create a template; then trace the hammer shape onto a piece of white poster board. Also trace the hammerhead onto black construction paper two times. Cut out the shapes. Glue one black hammerhead cutout to each side of the poster-board cutout. While the glue is drying, use colorful markers to decorate both sides of the handle. Attach a two-inch strip of magnetic tape to the back of the project. Then turn the project over. Write "#1 Dad" in white crayon on the hammerhead, and use craft glue (or a hot glue gun) to attach a wooden clothespin to the handle as shown. To create notepaper, press a finger onto a brightly colored stamp pad before pressing it onto 4" x 5" sheets of blank white paper. Use colorful fine-tipped markers to transform each fingerprint into a personalized work of art. Then stack and clip the decorated papers to the note holder. How nice!

Linda C. Buerklin—Substitute Teacher
Monroe Township Schools
Williamstown, NJ

Pencil-And-Paper Present

Here's a pointed suggestion that's just right for Father's Day gift giving. To begin, seal a legal-size envelope. With the back of the envelope faceup and the envelope turned vertically, fold and crease the lower corners to create a point. Tape the folds in place. Trim along the upper envelope edge, rounding the corners and opening the envelope. Wrap a 1" x 10" strip of construction paper around the envelope about one-fourth of the way down from the opening. Glue this band in place. Sketch vertical lines, scalloped lines, and a lead line similar to those shown. Then color the pencil design as desired. Use a white art pencil or correction pen to draw a smiling face on the pencil lead. Program the pencil with an appropriate Father's Day greeting. Recycle scrap paper and make it into a 4" x 6 1/2" notepad. Slide the notepad into the pencil-shaped envelope along with a brief Father's Day message and a new pencil or two. Tape or staple the open end of the envelope closed.

Splash!

Encourage your students to dive into this aquatic art idea. To make one of these art projects, begin with two sheets of white construction paper. Tear along the width of one of the sheets to create a wavy edge. Place the torn paper on a sheet of newspaper; then use colored chalk to heavily color the torn edge. Near the bottom of the other sheet of construction paper, place the torn-paper edge, chalk-side up. Using a facial tissue, work your way across the length of the chalk-covered tear, making repetitive downward strokes that smear the chalk onto the bottom sheet of paper. Repeat the process several times by again chalking the torn edge, placing

the torn paper higher on the other sheet than before, and smearing the chalk downward. When the bottom sheet has lots of chalky waves, it's time to add an aquatic animal. Partially unfold a paper clip to a 45° angle or less. Tape half of the clip to the back of a paper fish or sea creature and the other half to the sheet of wave designs. Is it just your imagination, or does that fish really appear to be swimming?

Julie Potts—Gr. 2, Cleveland Elementary, Elkhart, IN

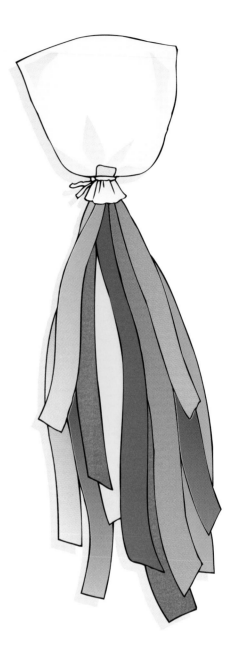

Rainbow Jellies

Make a splash with this seaworthy jellyfish project! Each child needs a gallon-size, clear, plastic food-storage bag; a twist-tie; and eight to ten 1 1/2" strips of tissue paper in a variety of lengths and colors. Align one end of the tissue-paper strips and hold that end of the stack in one hand. Hold the bag in your other hand. Blow air inside the bag to slightly inflate it; then quickly slip the aligned strip ends inside the bag, pinch the bag closed, and secure it with the twist-tie. To suspend the project, carefully tape a length of monofilament line to the bag. Easy to make, extremely colorful, and no poisonous punch—it's a perfect jellyfish!

Michele Converse Baerns
Sieverville Elementary
Sieverville, TN

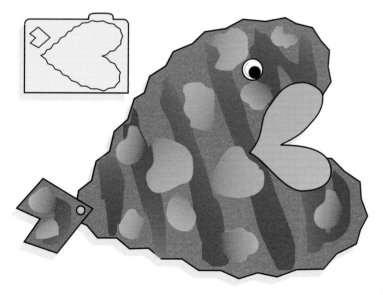

Fishy Fanfare

Fish lips! There *is* something fishy about this colorful swimmer, isn't there? To make a one-of-a-kind fish, use templates like the ones pictured to trace a fish body and tail onto one half of a discarded manila file folder. Cut on the resulting outlines. Working atop a newspaper-covered surface, use tempera paint to paint the cutouts a solid color. When this coat of paint has thoroughly dried, paint a two-color, tempera-paint design on the cutouts. Set the cutouts aside to dry. Later use a brad fastener to attach the fish tail to the fish body; then attach a wiggle eye, a pair of irresistible construction-paper lips, and other desired features. Too cute!

Kimberly Faraci—Gr. 1
Public School 19, Brooklyn, NY

Stylish Swimmers

Anything goes when it comes to fish fashion—especially when the fish are made from coffee filters! To make a stylish swimmer, submerge a coffee filter in a pan of shallow water; then lay the filter on a paper towel. Next use colorful markers to draw stripes and/or dots on the coffee filter. The colors will bleed, creating a unique design. When the filter is dry, trace a fish shape onto the filter (see the patterns on page 108) and cut it out. Add desired details with a black fine-tipped marker. The fish look lovely displayed in a window. Or they can be incorporated into an underwater scene like the one described below.

For added razzle-dazzle that's reminiscent of the remarkable rainbow fish (from *The Rainbow Fish* by Marcus Pfister), use a silver glitter pen, glue and silver glitter, or glue and a silver sequin to add a small shiny scale to the fish.

Shelley Cignoli—Gr. 1 Teacher Assistant
Jupiter Farms Community Elementary
Jupiter, FL

Underwater Seascapes

Whether you're wrapping up an ocean study or investigating coral reefs, make plans to create these colorful underwater scenes. To create the watery backdrop, cover a 9" x 12" sheet of white art paper with a length of plastic wrap. Using blue tempera, paint the portion of the plastic wrap that covers the art paper. Next slide the art paper from beneath the wrap and lay it on the painted surface. Use the palm of your hand to carefully press the paper against the plastic so the paint transfers to the paper. Then peel the paper from the plastic wrap. Set the art paper aside to dry, and dispose of the plastic. When the backdrop is dry, use torn construction paper and construction-paper cutouts (see the optional fish patterns on page 108) to create a colorful underwater scene.

Melanie J. Miller
Nashport, OH

75

Deep-Sea Extravaganza

Make a splash with these underwater habitats! To begin, cut the center from a paper plate. Use the resulting circle cutout as a guide for cutting a slightly larger circle from a scrap of laminating film. Secure the film cutout inside the paper-plate frame with masking tape. Set this portion of the project aside.

Use crayons to color the center of a second paper plate to resemble a backdrop for an underwater habitat. Brush a thin coat of glue over the resulting habitat floor and sprinkle sand over the glue. Allow drying time; then shake off the excess sand. If desired, glue a few pieces of aquarium gravel atop the sandy area. Next cut out and glue construction-paper fish, coral, starfish, greenery, and other desired elements to the underwater habitat. For a 3-D effect, fringe and/or bend forward parts of each cutout before gluing it in place. To assemble the project, staple the outer edges of the two paper plates together as shown.

Betty Jean Kobes—Multiage
West Hancock Elementary School
Kanawha, IA

Gone Fishin'

Youngsters will fall for this comical and creative project—hook, line, and sinker! To make a translucent fish, begin by cutting three 3-inch squares from black construction paper. Cut one of the squares along the diagonal, creating two triangles. Stack and fold the two squares. Starting at the fold, cut within the paper's perimeter so that two 1/4-inch square frames remain when the paper is unfolded and separated. Repeat this process with the triangles, creating two identical triangular frames. Remove the backing from a piece of clear Con-Tact® covering and place it sticky side up on a tabletop. Arrange a square frame and a triangular frame to resemble a fish shape. Press torn or cut tissue-paper pieces onto the Con-Tact paper to colorize the areas inside the frames. Add tissue-paper pieces outside the frames to resemble fins. Place the remaining frames atop the first ones. Cut out a black paper eye and place it on the tissue paper. Use a second sheet of Con-Tact paper to seal the pieces in place. Cut around the fish, leaving a thin margin of Con-Tact covering around the outside of the fish.

For a display that makes the fish seem to swim, attach thread to the fish and hang it from the ceiling. Or encourage students to add to the whimsy by suspending several fish and a hooked-worm cutout (see page 109) from a poster-board bobber. Four or five of your fishing enthusiasts may enjoy incorporating their fish into a single mobile.

Folding sample:

Underwater Mobile

Make a splash with this aquatic art project! Draw and brightly color a large fish on a six-inch square of drawing paper. Cut out the fish, color its blank side, and hole-punch the top of the cutout. Using circle templates, trace and cut out a seven-inch and a six-inch circle from blue or green construction paper. Make a spiral cut to the center of each circle, pull each resulting spiral upward, and hole-punch its center. Tie one end of a length of ribbon or string to each cutout; then tie the loose ribbon ends to a plastic drinking straw. Tie one end of a fourth ribbon length near the center of the straw. Suspend the completed mobile and watch the colorful fish swim in the springtime breezes.

Carolyn Williams—Gr. 2
North Augusta Elementary
North Augusta, SC

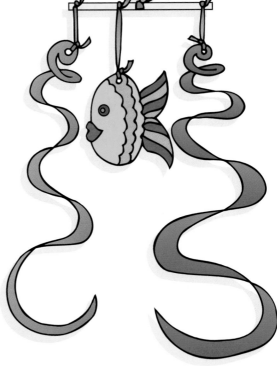

spiral cut

Red, White, And Blue

Plan to make these patriotic windsocks for a July 4th celebration. Even if your school year ends in June, students will enjoy making the decorations for their upcoming family celebrations. To make a patriotic windsock, glue several white construction-paper star cutouts onto a 6" x 18" strip of blue construction paper. Roll the star-studded strip of paper into a cylinder and glue the overlapping edges together. Next glue eight to ten 16-inch strips of crepe paper (alternating red and white lengths) along the lower edge of the project. To prepare the windsock for hanging, punch two holes near the top of the cylinder so that the holes are on opposite sides of the project. Thread each end of a 36-inch length of yarn or string through a different hole and securely tie. Happy birthday, America!

adapted from an idea by Rita Arnold—Grs. K–5 Learning Disabilities Teacher
Alden-Hebron Elementary School
Hebron, IL

Dots By The Droves

Here's a dot. There's a dot. Everywhere there are dots—more dots! Most of the time an ordinary dot is not thought of as an art tool. But skillful artists have proven that the dot can be as powerful a force in art-work as can a brush stroke. Have your youngsters try their hands at artwork comprised of dots, called *pointillism.* To make a pointillistic picture, begin by drawing a simple design with a marker. Dip a cotton swab in tempera paint and repeatedly press the swab end onto the paper, filling an area of the design with dots. Use additional swabs and other colors of tempera paint to fill the remaining areas of the design. As you work, remember that—from a distance—dots that are placed closer together appear to create darker areas than dots of the same color that are more loosely scattered.

Joan Mary Macey—Art Teacher, Benjamin Franklin School
Binghamton, NY

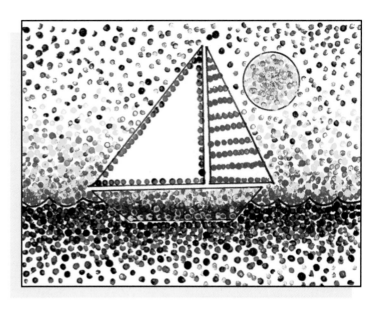

Sunset Silhouettes

To make this impressive sunset, align an 8" x 11" piece of manila paper atop an 8" x 11" piece of white construction paper and staple the two top corners. At the bottom, tear off a narrow strip of the manila paper. Pressing heavily, draw a chalk line along the torn paper edge; then use a facial tissue to rub the chalk downward onto the exposed portion of the white paper. When this step has been completed, tear off another narrow strip of manila paper and repeat the process, using a different color of chalk and a clean portion of tissue. Continue in this manner until you have used the last strip of manila paper. Then remove the staples and the remaining manila paper. Smear the top chalk layer upward to cover any white space at the top of the page. Cut a desired silhouette from black paper and glue it on your colorful sun-set. Mount the project on a 9" x 12" sheet of black construction paper.

Karen Saner—Grs. K–1
Burns Elementary School
Burns, KS

Blue-Ribbon Bouquet

Do the environment a favor by having your students recycle plastic six-pack rings into eye-catching imitation daisies. Once your students have made a few dozen of these blooms (according to the directions that follow), use the flowers in a number of ways. Have students arrange daisies and some silk greenery in flowerpots fitted with Styrofoam® and decorated with foil and bows. Place these pots on your windowsill or around the podium at an end-of-the-year assembly to add a sunny touch. Or have each student tie a ribbon around a flower that he made, write a personal note to someone on the faculty or staff, and deliver the flower with his wishes for a pleasant summer. There's no time like the present to say it with flowers!

Becky Gibson Watson, Camp Hill, AL

In advance collect the following items:
—plastic six-pack rings from soft drinks (a minimum of two per student)
—16-gauge floral wire (a minimum of one foot per student)
—old pens with sharp points for punching holes in the rings
—cardboard (for protecting the work surfaces)
—pliers, wire cutters, or scissors for cutting floral wire
—spray paint for tinting the flower petals
—green floral tape
—buttons or pom-poms for the flower centers
—scissors for student use
—green construction paper
—glue

Instructions:
1. To prepare the six-pack rings for use, have youngsters trim each six-pack ring to create six circular rings.
2. To make a daisy, begin by pinching opposite sides of a ring until they touch in the middle. Place the middle of the pinched ring on a piece of cardboard. Press the point of an old pen through both thicknesses of the plastic, creating two small holes. Repeat this process with at least seven additional rings.
3. Thread the rings onto a 12"–16" length of floral wire, arranging each ring at a different angle.
4. Bunch the rings near one end of the wire, and bend less than 1/2" of the wire to make a loop that will hold the rings in place so that they resemble the petals of a flower.
5. Take the imitation flower and the spray paint outside. Spray-paint the plastic rings, taking care not to paint the wire (flower stem).
6. Cut out green construction-paper leaves with stems.
7. Use floral tape to attach each leaf's stem securely to the floral wire.
8. Glue a button or pom-pom to the flower's center.

Roly-Poly Owls

Who-o-o-o-o could resist these adorable paper-bag owls? Use the patterns on page 107 to create tagboard templates for the outer and inner faces, the eyes, and the beak. Use a pencil to trace the outer face template on brown paper, the inner face template on black paper, the eye template on green paper (twice), and the beak template on orange paper. Use a black marker to trace over the pencil lines and to add a black pupil inside each eye shape. Cut out and assemble the patterns as shown. Next glue the resulting owl face to the bottom of an unfolded brown lunch bag. Allow drying time; then carefully stuff the lunch bag with crumpled newspaper or scrap paper. Use a black pipe cleaner to securely tie the bottom of the bag. Fashion a talon from each pipe-cleaner end as shown. "Hoot-diggity"! That's a fine-looking owl!

Carrie Tetson Geiger, Gainesville, FL

Native American Moments

If your youngsters are learning about Native American culture, then this art project is an open-ended culminating activity you won't want to miss. Ask each youngster to recall one group of Native Americans to feature in his artwork. Help him in recalling the lay of the land on which this group lives or previously lived. Encourage him to recall the types of shelters and activities that were or are indicative of the Native Americans that he has chosen. Then guide each student in developing a collage.

In preparation for making a collage, thin glue with water. Brush the thinned glue onto a large sheet of art paper. Place strips of tissue paper on the glue so that they overlap, creating a sky-and-landscape background. Brush on more thinned glue if necessary. Cut dwellings, people, and other objects from construction paper and glue them on top of the tissue-paper background. If desired, crayon or marker details can be added to the collage when it dries. Your students will love the vivid results!

Rebecca English—Gr. 2
Dawson County Primary School
Dawsonville, GA

Puzzle-Piece Picture Frame

Puzzled about what kinds of gifts students can make for parents and other important adults? This fun frame is a perfect fit!

Materials For One Picture Frame:
one 12" length of decorative tinsel wire or narrow ribbon
one 6" x 8" piece of clear plastic mesh
1 student photo
1 piece of clear Con-Tact® covering twice the size of the photo
one 8" x 10" piece of clear plastic wrap
70 to 80 jigsaw-puzzle pieces
craft glue

1. Attach the tinsel wire to a short end of the plastic mesh by tying the ends of the wire to the outermost corners of the mesh.
2. Cover the student photo with the Con-Tact® covering.
3. Place the plastic mesh atop the piece of clear plastic wrap; then glue the photo in the center of the plastic mesh.
4. Glue a layer of puzzle pieces around the photo, creating a border.
5. Glue a second and a third layer of puzzle pieces around the photo until the edges of the photo and the plastic mesh can not be seen.

Linda Mates—Gr. 2, Public School 206, Brooklyn, NY

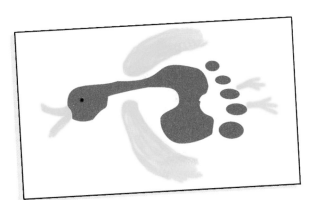

Footprint Fowl

These one-of-a-kind fliers will bring your students to their feet! Protect an area of the classroom floor with newspapers. Into a dishpan pour a thin layer of tempera paint and liquid soap mixture. (Prepare one dishpan for each desired paint color.) To make the body of his bird, a youngster puts his bare foot into a dishpan of paint, then presses his paint-covered footprint onto the center of a sheet of white construction paper. Then, using a contrasting color of paint and a paintbrush, he creates his bird's wing(s) and any desired scenery. The following day, when the paint has dried, each student uses markers to draw details like eyes, a beak, and feet.

Janette E. Anderson—Substitute Teacher Grs. K–3
Fremont School District, Fremont, CA

Tissue-Paper Banners

These colorful tissue-paper banners are a cut above the rest! Begin with a length of tissue paper that measures approximately 10" x 18". To create a casing, fold the top one inch of the tissue paper forward (Step 1); then accordion-fold the tissue at two-inch intervals (Step 2). Cut a series of shapes along one side of the project, taking care to not cut through the casing (Step 3). Unfold the project. Display the colorful banners end-to-end along lengths of suspended string or yarn. To do this, slip the string under the casing; then tape the casing closed (Step 4). With these banners in place, your classroom ambience will be full of cheer—and color!

Ruth Trinidad—Gr. 1, 28th Street School
Los Angeles, CA

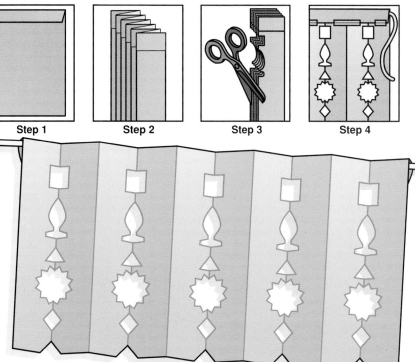

Step 1   Step 2   Step 3   Step 4

Water Lily Masterpieces

Expect lots of passersby to stop and admire these striking water lily projects. Nearly fill a large aluminum pan with water. Sparingly dribble a few drops of blue oil-base paint into the water. Use a craft stick to swirl the paint. Place a sheet of art paper on the surface of the water; then lift it from the water using tongs. When the paint has dried completely (which may be several days later depending on the paint and the humidity), cut irregular oval-like shapes from green construction paper. Glue the green shapes on the painted paper to represent water lilies. Fold a coffee filter in half repeatedly until it resembles a narrow wedge. Trim the wedge as shown. Unfold the filter, gather and twist it at the center bottom, and glue or staple it to a water lily. Add additional coffee-filter blooms as desired to complete the masterpiece.

Wow, What Weavings!

Here's an interesting twist on a traditional idea. To make one of these projects, begin by folding a sheet of construction paper in half (to a 6" x 9" size). Near the fold, use a ruler and pencil to mark the paper at one-inch intervals. With scissors, cut from the fold at each mark to within one-inch of the opposite paper edge. Unfold the paper. Weave contrasting 1" x 9" strips in and out of the slits in the construction paper until the entire sheet is woven. Trim and glue the strip ends. Use a template to trace a distinctive outline of your choice onto a sheet of dark construction paper. Punch a scissors blade into the center of the outline; then cut to and around the outline, leaving an uncut piece of construction paper around the open area. Glue the frame to the woven sheet and display. Quite a few people will do double takes as they try to figure out how your students achieved such interesting visual effects.

Allison Pratt
Winona, MN

Paper-Plate Snake

Snakes alive! Have you ever seen such a colorful snake? To begin cut the rim from a thin, white paper plate. Set aside the circular center of the plate and cut the resulting piece of rim in half. Glue together the two pieces of rim so that they form an *S*. To make the snake's head, make a cut from the exterior of the circle piece to its center point. Overlap the resulting edges and glue. Trim to create a desired snake head shape; then glue the snake head to the snake body. Decorate the snake as desired using colorful tempera paint. Could this be a rain-forest snake? Or maybe Jimmy's boa is on the loose!

Kathy Compton—Grs. 1–2, Browning Primary, Royse City, TX

Debonair Ducks

Create a pond full of majestic male mallard ducks in a matter of minutes! Start with one-half of a paper plate. Use brown tempera paint to sponge-print the outside of the plate; then set the plate aside to dry. Trim a 4 1/2" x 6" piece of dark green construction paper to resemble a duck's head and neck. Create an eye on the duck head and glue a thin, white paper ring to the mallard's neck. Cut a duck bill from a three-inch square of yellow construction paper and attach it to the duck head. Then glue the duck head to the duck body as shown. Display these dapper ducks paddling across a large paper pond. Quack! Quack!

Tissue-Paper Impressions

Small scraps of colored tissue paper make a big impact on these one-of-a-kind creations. Choose scraps of tissue paper with which to decorate a 5" x 8" sheet of white construction paper. Trim the scraps if necessary and arrange them on the paper. Using water and a small paintbrush, dampen each piece of tissue paper and gently press it into place. Then brush over the arrangement using a glaze of two parts white glue and one part water. When the paper is dry, mount it atop a 6" x 9" sheet of colorful construction paper.

Amy Butler Barsanti—Gr. 1
St. Hilda's and St. Hugh's School
New York, NY

Winsome Wind Chimes

They say one person's trash is another person's treasure. Without a doubt your young recyclists will take great pride in these unique wind chimes. To make a wind chime, begin by collecting and cleaning nine metal juice-can lids. Use a hammer and a nail to poke a hole near the rim of each lid. Paint both sides of each of the lids with a dark color of tempera paint to which a few drops of liquid detergent have been added. If the wind chimes will be hung outdoors, use clear acrylic spray to coat both sides of the lids. Tie a length of string to each lid. Then attach the lids at varying heights from a four-inch embroidery-hoop ring or similar substitute. Use ribbon to suspend the ring so that it will hang parallel to the floor. Who would have thought juice-can lids could be so eye-catching and melodious?

Linda Schwitzke, Longview, WA

Foil Fanfare

For lots of razzle-dazzle, get creative with foil and permanent markers. To make this project, crumple a piece of foil; then flatten it, leaving it somewhat crinkled. Using a black permanent marker, draw a large shape on the foil. Inside the shape, draw smaller, yet similar shapes. Color the shapes using permanent color markers. (If colorful permanent markers are not available, add a few drops of food coloring to each of several small containers of white glue. Paint each shape with a thin coat of tinted glue.) Cut out and mount the project on black construction paper; then trim the black paper to create an eye-catching border.

Darlene Hennessy—Substitute Teacher
Tacoma School District
Tacoma, WA

Critter Cages

Here's a 3-D project your youngsters will be wild about. Fold in half a 6" x 8" sheet of black construction paper so that the folded paper measures 6" x 4". Use a ruler to draw parallel lines from the fold to within an inch of the opposite edges, spacing the lines about 1/2 inch apart. Cut on the lines. To create a cagelike effect, unfold the black paper to a 90° angle; then bend and crease every other strip in the opposite direction from the fold. Next fold a 6" x 5" piece of white paper in half to 3" x 5". Starting at the fold, cut two parallel lines about one inch apart. Unfold the paper to a 90° angle; then bend and crease the resulting strip in the opposite direction from the original fold. Decorate the paper as desired, before gluing it inside the black paper cage. Next color and cut out a critter to fit inside the cage. Glue the cutout to the front of the protruding white strip.

To display the completed project, accordion-fold a 9" x 12" sheet of construction paper into three equal sections. Unfold the top flap to a 90° angle and sandwich the cage inside by aligning the fold lines. Glue the project in place; then secure the bottom flap with a dab of glue.

Kathy Radford, Pleasant Valley Elementary, Winfield, KS

Geometric Wonders

If you know the right moves, delightful geometric designs can be made in a jiffy! To begin, use tape to secure a sheet of white paper to a slightly larger piece of corrugated cardboard. Next use a pushpin to hold one corner of a desired geometric tagboard template in place. Trace around the shape with a colored pencil; then, keeping the pushpin in place, slightly rotate the shape and retrace its outline with a different colored pencil. Continue rotating and tracing the shape, using as many or as few colors of pencils as desired. When the shape has been completely rotated, the drawing is complete. Remove the paper from the cardboard, crop the colorful design, and mount it on a slightly larger piece of construction paper. These colorful creations will be popping up all over the place!

Valerie Smith, Exton, PA

Colorful Crayons

Create a rainbow of color and promote class unity with these jumbo crayons! As a prelude to the project, discuss the meaning of the phrase "It takes every color to make the rainbow." Help students understand how this phrase applies to their classroom, their community, and their world. Then begin the project with a 6" x 18" piece of white construction paper and a supply of colorful tissue-paper squares. Using diluted glue and a paintbrush, "paint" the tissue-paper squares onto the paper, overlapping the squares as you cover the rectangle. When the rectangle is completely covered, set it aside to dry. The following day trim a 4" x 6" piece of construction paper to resemble the point of a crayon and glue it to one end of the tissue paper–covered rectangle. To the opposite end glue a 2 1/2" x 6" piece of construction paper. Then personalize a construction-paper oval (or other desired shape) and glue it to the side of the crayon. Mount the completed projects on a bulletin board titled "It Takes Every Color To Make The Rainbow."

Jennifer Balogh-Joiner—Gr. 2
Franklin Elementary School
Franklin, NJ

Edible Peanut-Butter Clay

Try this recipe for an afternoon of modeling fun and a tasty snack all in one! Mix your clay a day in advance so that it can be refrigerated overnight. To make enough clay for 25 to 27 students, mix 3 cups of peanut butter with 1 1/2 cups of honey. (Swirl 1 teaspoon of oil in the measuring cup before measuring the honey to keep it from sticking.) Stir in 4 1/2 cups of instant dry milk, a little at a time, until stiff. Knead the dough with your hands until well blended; then cover and store it in the refrigerator. The next day, give each youngster a piece of waxed paper and some peanut-butter clay. Each student molds his clay into a desired shape or shapes. Encourage students to view their classmates' peanut-butter sculptures; then let each child eat his own.

Here's Lookin' At You!

Generate a lot of enthusiasm for self-portraits using a secret ingredient—wiggle eyes. Introduce this activity by giving each student a pair of wiggle eyes. They are now available in several colors, so students may be given wiggle eyes that closely resemble the color of their own eyes. Provide mirrors and have students talk about the appearance of their eyes and the rest of their images. Ask each student to draw a self-portrait using the eyes, glue, markers, and a piece of tagboard. Label the back of each illustration with the name of the artist who rendered it. Then shuffle the pictures and ask students to identify the owner of each self-portrait.

Linda Yoffe—Art Teacher
Tokeneke School
Darien, CT

Daffy Daisy Heads

So what would you do if a daisy sprang from the top of your head? Follow up an oral reading of *Daisy-Head Mayzie* by Dr. Seuss with this kid-pleasing project. To make a daisy head, adorn a three-inch Styrofoam® ball with a crop of yellow yarn hair, two wiggle eyes, and a red pipe-cleaner smile. Poke the stem of a plastic daisy into the top of the resulting head; then rest the daisy head atop a decorated toilet-tissue tube. For a related writing activity, ask each child to pen a story about his daisy head's latest adventure!

Peggy Auvil—Gr. 3
Espy Elementary
Nixa, MO

93

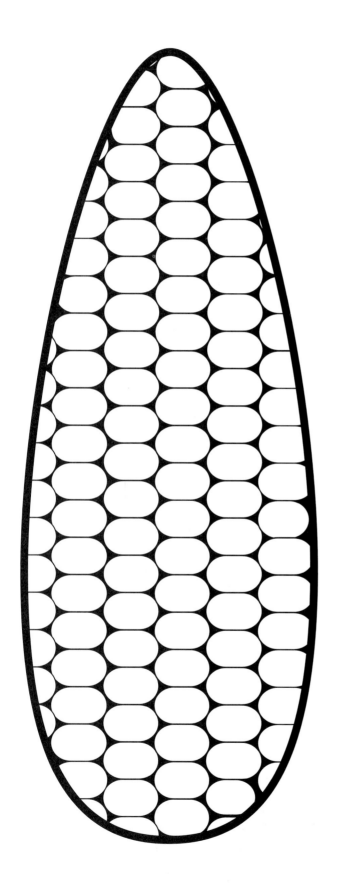
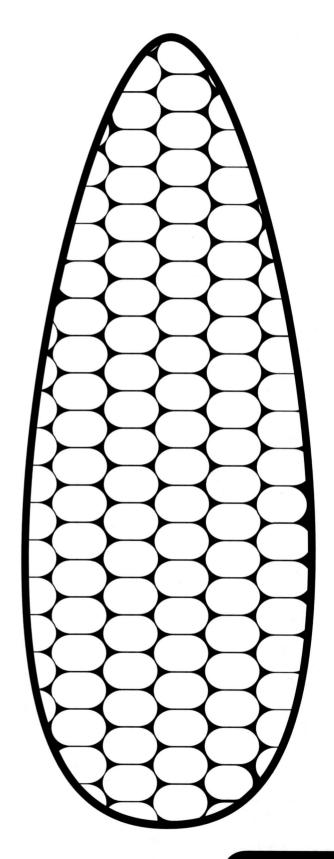

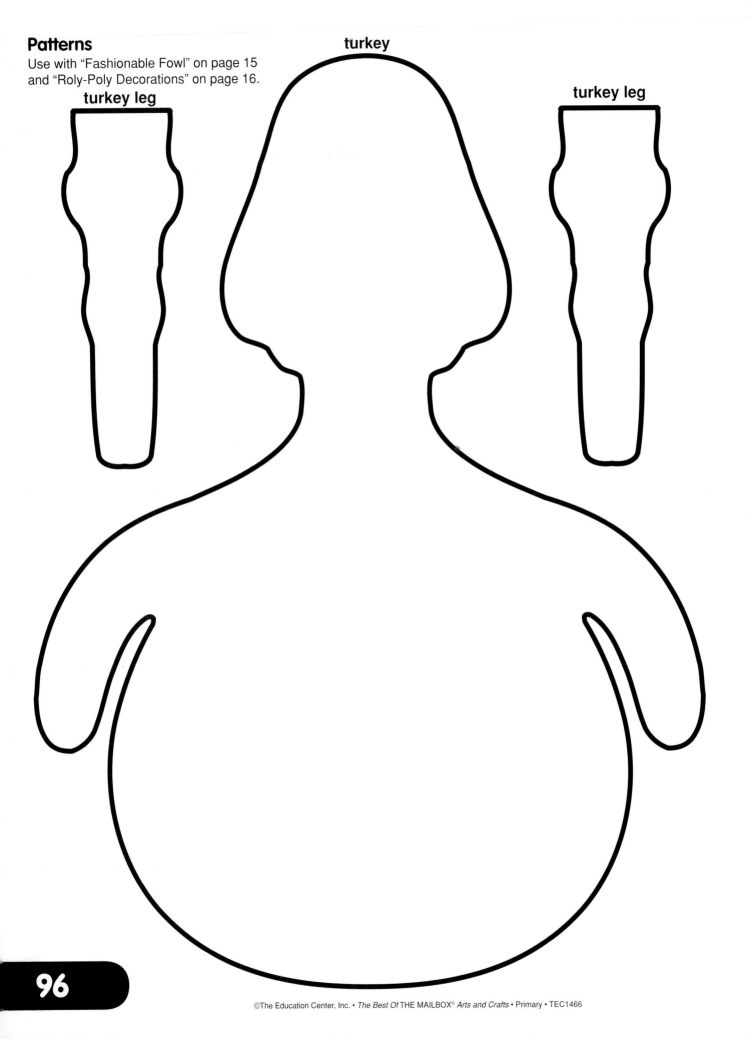

Patterns
Use with "Fashionable Fowl" on page 15
and "Roly-Poly Decorations" on page 16.

turkey leg

turkey

turkey leg

turkey

Patterns

Use the leaf and candle-flame patterns with "Crown Of Candles" on page 24.

Use the star patterns
with "Star-Studded Hat"
on page 24.

Patterns

Use with "Seasonal Symmetry" on page 27.

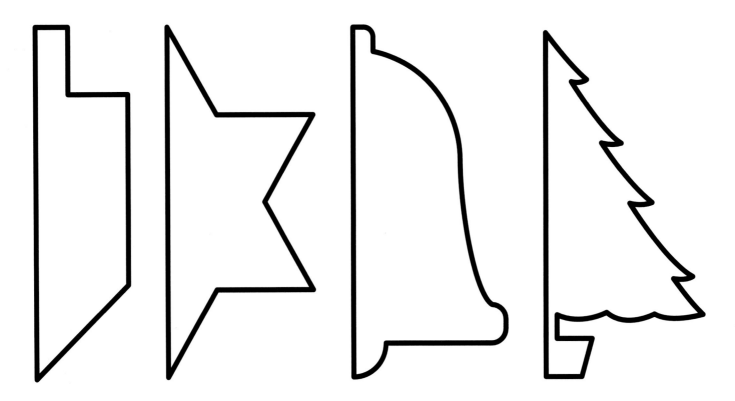

Use with "Rudolph Replicas" on page 29.

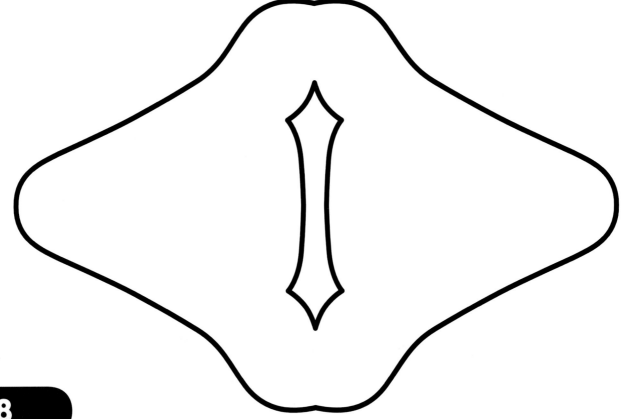

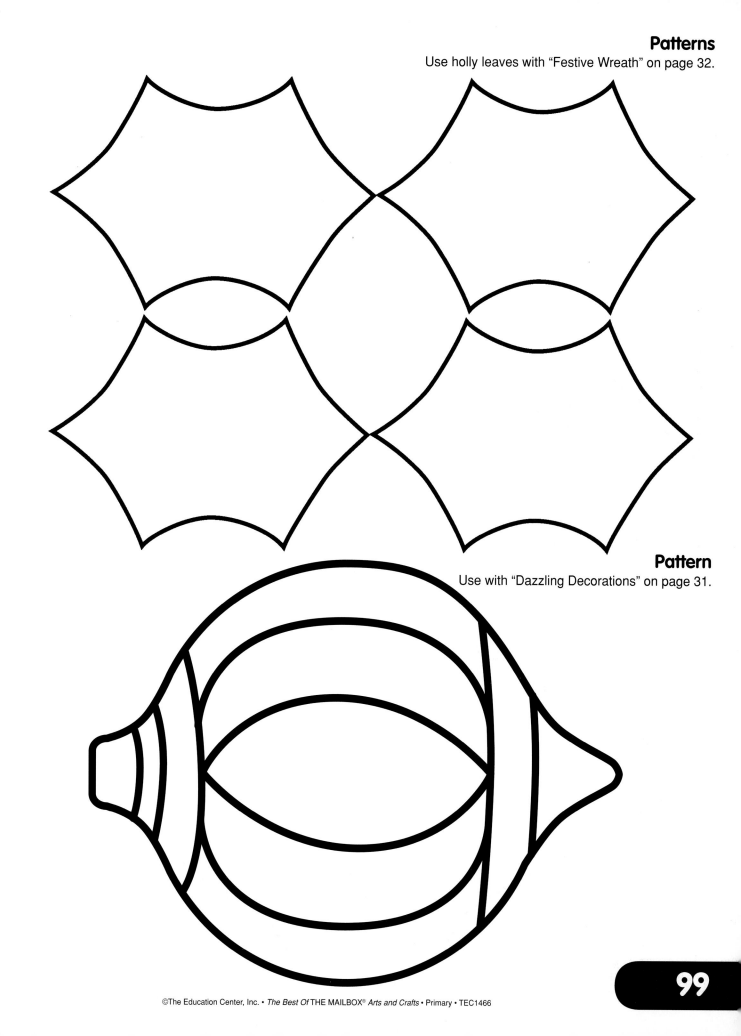

Pattern
Use with "Dazzling Decorations" on page 31.

101

Patterns
Use pattern and writing suggestions with
"Poetic Planter" on page 69.

Writing Suggestions:
Line 1: name of this person
Line 2: three present-tense verbs that tell actions of this person
Line 3: phrase telling where this person can be found
Line 4: another phrase telling where this person can be found
Line 5: another phrase telling where this person can be found
Line 6: a summarizing thought about this person

Patterns

Use with "Presidents' Windsock" and "Famous Folks" on page 47.

103

Glue here.

Place on fold.

Place on fold.

Resulting Tagboard Tracer

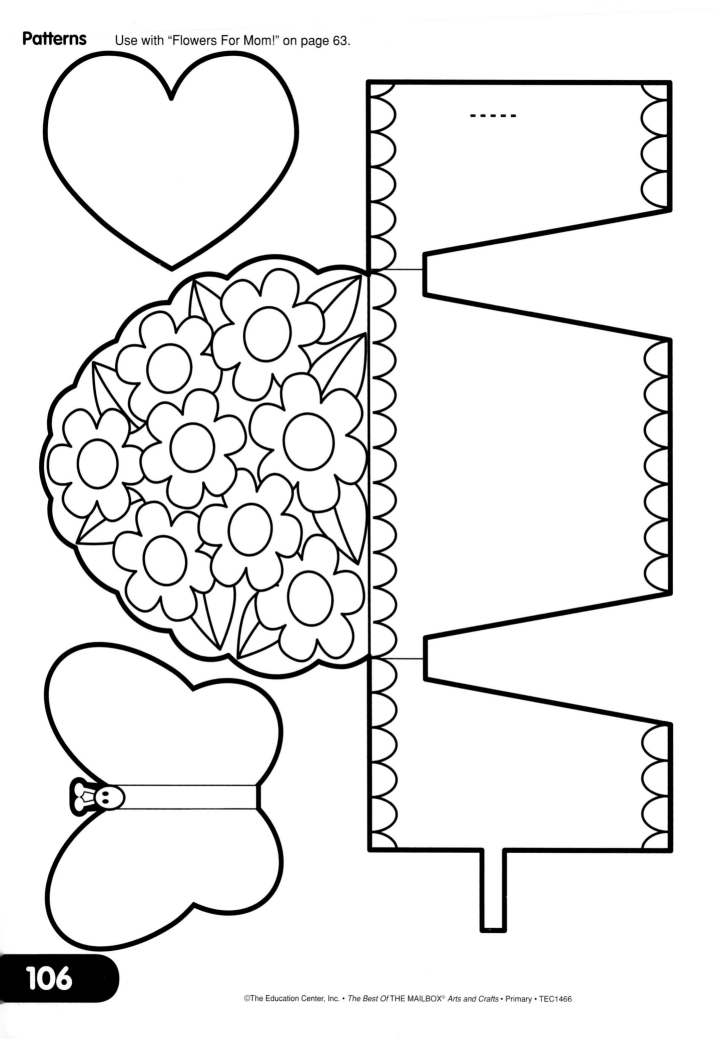

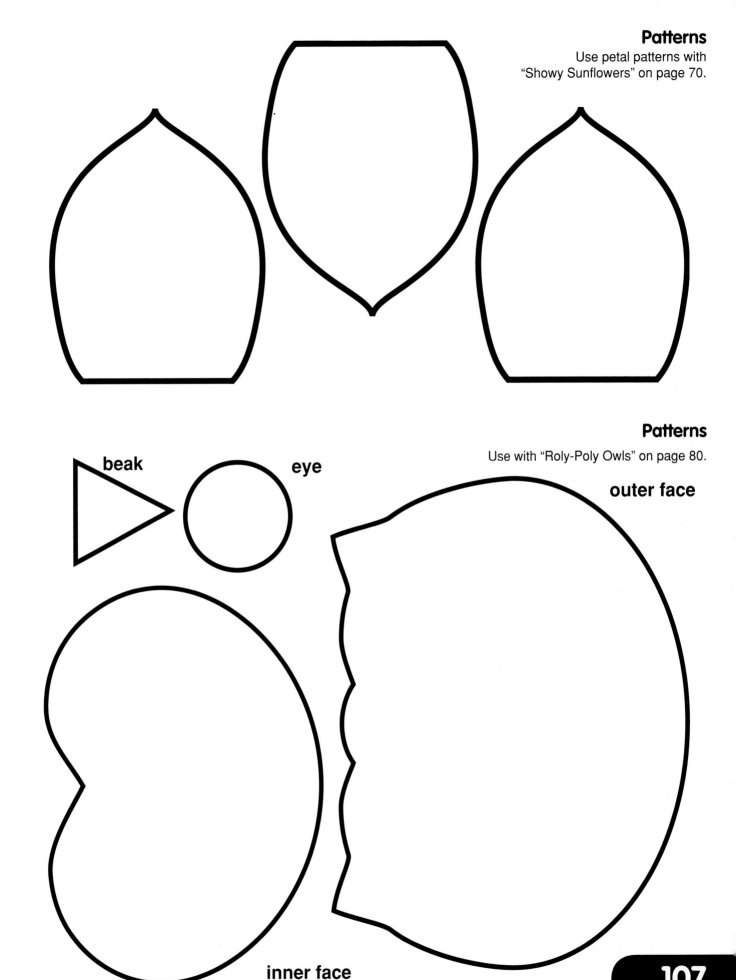

Patterns
Use petal patterns with
"Showy Sunflowers" on page 70.

Patterns
Use with "Roly-Poly Owls" on page 80.

outer face

beak

eye

inner face

107

Patterns

Use the fish patterns with
"Underwater Seascapes"
and "Stylish Swimmers"
on page 75.

Pattern

Use the hammer pattern
with "Magnetic Note
Holder" on page 72.

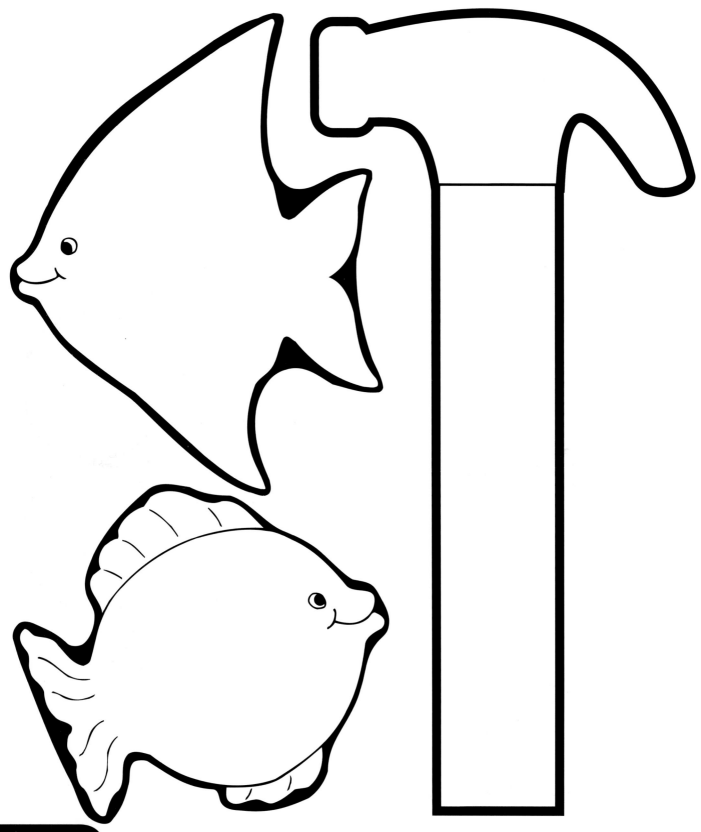

Hooked Worm Pattern

Use this pattern with "Gone Fishin' " on page 76 and the assembly instructions below.

Assembly Instructions For "Gone Fishin' " Mobile

1. Attach thread to the tops of several fish cutouts. See "Gone Fishin' " on page 76.
2. Cut out a bobber shape from poster board. Color the lower half of each side to resemble a bobber.
3. Color a paper copy of the designs below.
4. Fold the designs along the dotted fold line. Hold the folded paper up to the light to assure that the designs are correctly aligned. Then cut around the design.
5. Glue the two halves of the hooked-worm design together.
6. Attach thread to the top of the hook design and attach the other end of the thread to the bottom center of the bobber.
7. Suspend the fish cutouts from the bobber so that the mobile balances and the fish can rotate.

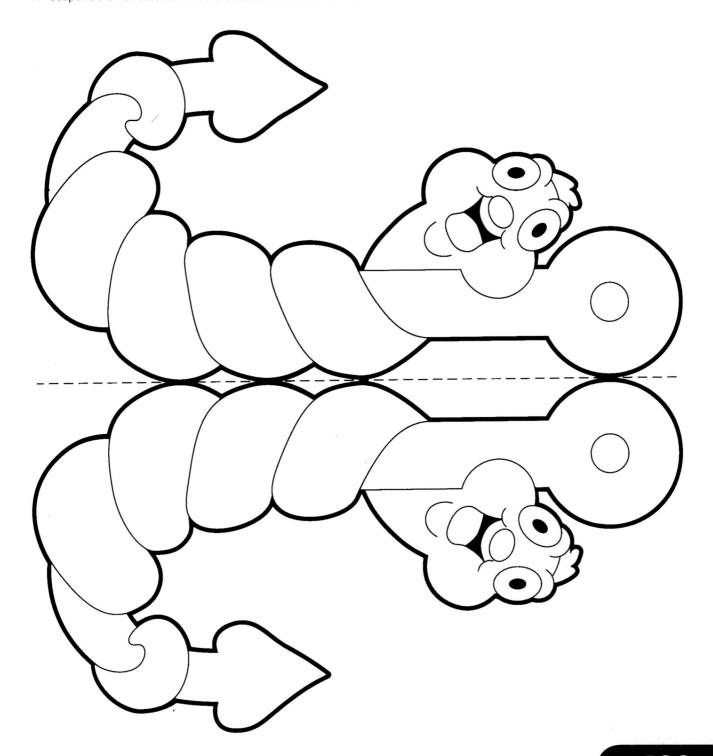

109

Index